Ancient Peoples and Places

PAGAN SCANDINAVIA

General Editor

DR. GLYN DANIEL

ABOUT THE AUTHOR

H. R. Ellis Davidson, who studied English, archaeology, and anthropology at Newnham College, Cambridge, became interested in the religion of pagan Scandinavia while working for her doctorate and has continued research on this and allied subjects ever since. She is a Fellow of the Society of Antiquaries and has lectured in English Literature and Language at the Royal Holloway College and Birkbeck College of the University of London. Mrs. Davidson has published many books and articles, among them The Sword in Anglo-Saxon England and Gods and Myths of Northern Europe, and is at present studying influences on the religion of the Viking Age that came from the East by way of Russia.

Ancient Peoples and Places

PAGAN SCANDINAVIA

H. R. Ellis Davidson

68 PHOTOGRAPHS
29 LINE DRAWINGS
1 MAP

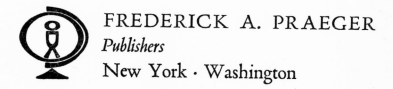

FREDERICK A. PRAEGER
Publishers
New York · Washington

THIS IS VOLUME FIFTY-EIGHT IN THE SERIES
Ancient Peoples and Places
GENERAL EDITOR: DR. GLYN DANIEL

BOOKS THAT MATTER

Published in the United States of America in 1967
by Frederick A. Praeger, Inc., Publishers,
111 Fourth Avenue, New York, N.Y. 10003
© 1967 by H. R. Ellis Davidson in London, England
All rights reserved
Library of Congress Catalog Card Number: 67-24530
Printed in Holland

CONTENTS

ILLUSTRATIONS

8

9

Foreword

THIS IS A SURVEY of archaeological evidence from Scandinavia which throws light on the religion of pagan times, and an attempt to break new ground. For many years scholars have worked exhaustively on the clues to be extracted from texts, inscriptions, philology and place names; more recently archaeologists and art historians have sought to interpret the evidence of material remains such as graves, sanctuaries, finds from bogs, carved stones, figurines, amulets and ornament. I have tried to summarize the results of archaeological findings in the light of what can be learned from the evidence of written sources, and have also taken into account the contribution from a third discipline, the history of religions, in which great progress has been made in recent years. Although I approached this task in some trepidation, I am most grateful to Dr Glyn Daniel and the publishers for inviting me to undertake it.

I am well aware of the dangers of such an approach as this, and of the temptation to read too much into isolated clues and ambiguous symbols – 'but one halfpennyworth of bread to this intolerable deal of sack.' Yet the opposite temptation too must be avoided, that of wearing pedantic blinkers within the safety of our own familiar fields, where we learn more and more about less and less, while the academic barriers between the disciplines rise ever higher as the scholarly output increases. This work is a tentative beginning to a history of religious symbolism in the Scandinavian North, and the fairly consistent pattern which emerges, incomplete although I know it to be, has led me to a greater understanding and respect for those nameless ones who have left a record of the rites which they practised, and of their instinctive or imaginative response as artists and craftsmen to the faith of their age. It is to them that I would wish, in all humility, to dedicate this book.

My thanks are due to the Trustees of the Leverhulme Research Awards, whose grant to me in 1964 for visits to museums in the Soviet Union, Helsinki and Stockholm enabled me to collect useful material. On these and subsequent visits, I received much help from scholars and museum staffs, specially from Dr Wencke Slomann of Universitets Oldsaksamling in Oslo, Professor Bertil Almgren of the University of Uppsala, and the Director and staff of Gotlands Fornsal in Visby. I am grateful also for assistance from the National Museum of Denmark, the Statens Historiska Museum and the Museum Archives in Stockholm, as well as the museums of Bergen and Trondheim. Others who have been most generous in supplying photographs are the Directors of the museums at Lund and Schleswig, the Director of the Manx Museum in Douglas, Isle of Man, Mrs Leslie Webster of the British Museum, Mrs Sonia Hawkes, Count Eric Oxenstierna, and the Librarian of the Society of Antiquaries, Mr J. H. Hopkins, who is a never-failing help in times of trouble. To Mr Peter Gelling I owe thanks for reading and commenting on this book in its early stages, and to Dr Glyn Daniel for his helpful criticism. I greatly appreciate the work done by Miss Gillian Jones on the drawings and Miss Lucinda Rodd on the map; also the help given by Mrs Iris Merchant with the latter and the plans. Once more I am indebted to my husband for untiring support and interest.

H.R.E.D.

CHAPTER I

The Threshold of Religion

It is necessary to treat the animals well, and to regard all things as if they were living beings who hear and understand.

JOHAN TURI, *Muittalus Samid Birra.*

INTRODUCTION

EVIDENCE FOR THE BELIEFS of early man in a super-natural world must necessarily be fragmentary and suggestive. Survival from prehistoric times is largely a matter of accident, and we must not therefore read too much into isolated hints of ritual and ceremonial. Even when there are clear traces of this, a gap remains between the rites and the beliefs which inspired them, so that without the evidence of language to help us we may feel that the door is forever closed to the religious world of early man. Some archaeologists have indeed declared as much. Yet surely certain windows remain open, through which we can catch glimpses of this lost world.

Something may be learned from the rites and practices of primitive hunting communities, for although it is rash to press analogies too far, they can reveal to us the mental world of the early hunters, where small isolated communities wandered in search of food, with the constant risk of violent death or starvation. It becomes clear that such people live close to the animal world, with a clarity of observation denied to men in more developed civilizations. We can learn also of the relationship between ritual and the crafts of daily life, the constant use of symbolism, and the emphasis placed on the turning points of man's existence, which are birth, puberty, marriage and death. Much also can be learned by the use of other disciplines outside archaeology, and indeed without these there is a danger of making wild and misleading assumptions from the very little evidence which archaeology provides. It is essential to know something of the pattern of religious development in primitive communities in different regions of the world if we are to get our proportions right, and there is now much evidence available from both hemispheres. While there is no room in this book to present such evidence in detail, reference may be made to works on religion and symbolism given in the Bibliography (pages 149-151). When the Scandinavian evidence is seen against this larger background, it takes on clearer significance.

Archaeology brings home one point which historians of religion sometimes forget: the enormous length of time during which man lived by hunting in Northern Europe, measured not in centuries but by millennia. The religious beliefs of this vast period must have etched themselves deeply into his mind and spirit. While the range of archaeology is limited, it can provide evidence for certain established behaviour patterns that divide early man from the animal world with which he was still closely linked. First, there were rites showing man's rela-

Fig. 1   Map showing principal archaeological sites

1 *Sagelva*	17 *Birka*	33 *Tollund*
2 *Fykanvatn*	18 *Skedemose*	34 *Dejbjerg*
3 *Rødøy*	19 *Simrishamn*	35 *Egtved*
4 *Solsem*	02 *Kivik*	36 *Jelling*
5 *Evenhus*	21 *Karingsjön*	37 *Skrydstrup*
6 *Strand*	22 *Nämforsen*	38 *Haderslev*
7 *Vingen*	23 *St Hammars*	39 *Nydam*
8 *Borre*	24 *Sanda*	40 *Vimose*
9 *Oseberg*	25 *Tjängvide*	41 *Illerup*
10 *Gokstad*	26 *Buttle*	42 *Hjortspring*
11 *Tune*	27 *Kragehede*	43 *Trundholm*
12 *Sætrang*	28 *Gundestrup*	44 *Roskilde*
13 *Vendel*	29 *Borremose*	45 *Rude Eskildstrup*
14 *Valsgärde*	30 *Mammen*	46 *Grevens Vænge*
15 *Old Uppsala*	31 *Fårdal*	47 *Thorsbjerg*
16 *Tuna*	32 *Barkær*	

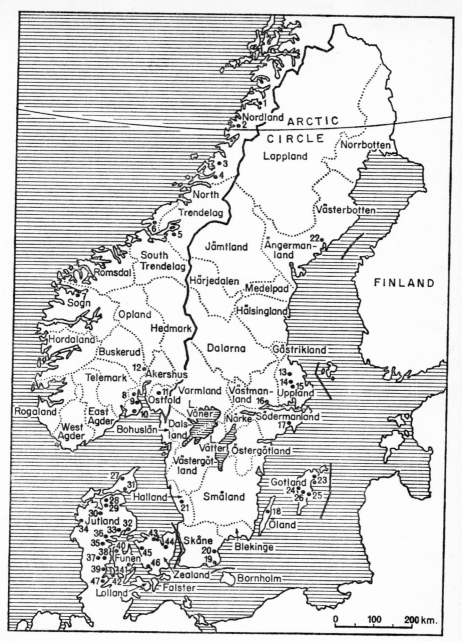

Fig. 1

tionship with animals, since growth of consciousness enabled him to realize this in a way denied to the animals themselves; these rites helped in hunting and in ensuring the continued supply of animal life. Secondly, there were rites showing interest in the dead, implying some conception of continued existence. Thirdly, there were offerings made to powers other than human, to propitiate them and seek their aid. In such behaviour patterns we may look for the beginnings of religion, and they form part of the larger body of evidence available for the beliefs of early man.

As long as Scandinavia was covered by ice it offered no opportunities for hunting and fishing communities to establish themselves, so that the first settlements are much later than further south. If little groups of Western Neanderthal stock wandered there in warmer periods between the Ice Ages, they have left no trace, and the only clue from the interglacial period in Denmark is a find of bones of fallow deer split to extract marrow, from a lake deposit near Hollerup. Evidence of ritual behaviour, such as is found in Neanderthal burial places elsewhere, is wholly lacking. Not until about 9000 BC do we find tools and weapons of stone and bone at early habitation sites such as Bromme in Denmark, sites round Ringsjö in Sweden, and Fosna in Norway. Their makers must have lived in small groups, as the Bushmen in South Africa have done up to our own time, continuing for thousands of years with little alteration in their way of life. Only an occasional hint of interest in anything more than the physical necessities of existence is afforded by the archaeological record.

At Stellmoor in Holstein, just across the Danish border, bodies of reindeer were thrown into a bog, and the skull of one animal put on a pole in the habitation site, suggesting sacrificial ritual. It must be assumed that this was not an isolated case, but that the most important animals, the reindeer, elk and bear, were sacrificed with ceremonial. Sacrificial ritual among hunting peoples in Siberia and the Ainu of Japan shows that they would seek forgiveness for the slaying of the bear which they so valued, honouring it with ceremonies and showing it affection so that it might return from the Other World in a state of benevolence towards them, and this is what we might assume took place at Stellmoor and elsewhere. There is clearer indication of man's interest and reverence for the animals that he hunted in the rock carvings of the Neolithic period.

THE ANIMALS ON THE ROCKS

Small animal sculptures surviving from the Early Neolithic period in Scandinavia show considerable artistic development, observation and skill. There are bone combs from Norway, which end in the head of elk or bird, spoons from eastern Scandinavia and slate knives from Helgeland with animal carvings, and small bone and amber figures of bears, seals and birds. Such art flourished among all the hunting peoples of Northern and Eastern Europe, and it is possible that some of the little figures had ritual significance. For example, an axe with a blunted edge, ending in the head of an elk, from Alunda, Uppland, may well have been used for sacrifice.

Plate 1

More definite evidence comes from the extensive rock carvings in Norway and Sweden. Over 70 sites are now known in Norway, and the number increases as new figures are discerned in remote places in the slanting light of the morning or evening sun. It was once thought that these carvings went back very early indeed, because of their resemblance to the Palaeolithic cave art of France and Spain. The tendency now, however, is to date their beginnings to the Middle Neolithic period, about 2000 BC, and to assume that they continued to be made until carvings of a different type superseded them in the Bronze Age, which in remote spots in the mountain areas of Norway may have come very late indeed. It is obviously very difficult to date any individual carving. At the most cautious estimate, they were produced for over a thousand years, and the finest examples are probably the result of a long period of development. There is no doubt that they satisfied a deep need in the life of the hunting communities.

One type of carving, and possibly the earliest one, takes the

Plate 2

form of a huge animal figure in silhouette, cut laboriously on the rock face. The method was to tap or prick out the outline with a hard, sharp stone on hard rock, or to cut deep, smooth furrows on softer rock. A few enormous figures in northern Norway are made by a honing and polishing technique, which has not worn as well as the others, but which must have been effective when new. The pictures were probably coloured, since traces of red, yellow and dark stains are sometimes visible in carvings in sheltered places.

These animal forms show the same mastery of technique and keen observation as the small animal sculptures. Often a characteristic pose is caught – a reindeer looking over its shoulder,

Fig. 2

the arching necks of wild swans, or line of elk in full gallop. The economy of line reveals an artistry of a very high order, although the richness of the finest Lascaux type of cave painting may be lacking. Often one animal is shown alone, but elk and reindeer are usually in pairs or small groups. The figures are in general much larger than life, one enormous whale at Leiknes being as much as 9 yards long.

A different, more stylized type of carving is found, in some cases alongside the first. While the naturalistic carvings are restricted mainly to elk, reindeer, stag, bear and fish, this second type includes more variety of subject. The stylized figures are diagrammatic, with straight lines and curves dividing up their bodies. The lines do not appear to indicate bone struc-

Plate 3

ture, and sometimes a line passes down the throat to end in a roughly circular shape inside the body, seemingly representing the heart or some vital organ. Sometimes the body is divided

Fig. 2   Outline of swans on rocks at Leiknes, near Tysfjord, Norway (after Hagen)

up into small compartments, or there are divisions which could indicate scales or feathers.

A third type of carving is even more schematic. This includes not only animals, birds and fishes, but also semi-human figures and inanimate objects such as boats, sledges and weapons, while geometric, abstract shapes are also found. A wall of rock covered with such figures resembles an artist's notebook, confused jottings and rough sketches being apparently added at random, some on top of others, yet all laboriously outlined in the solid rock. Clearly the intention behind such work differs from that which produced the majestic animals of the first type. Certain sites such as Vingen in Norway, with about 1500 figures, or Nämforsen in Sweden, with 200, show that the production of carvings went on over a long period.

Plate 4

It is now generally accepted that the purpose of such carvings was not purely aesthetic, a means of self-expression for the gifted hunter. Small sketches on bone or little carvings might be done for amusement, or practice, or to while away long periods of enforced inactivity, but these huge memorials must have had deeper significance for those who worked so hard to produce them. Where modern parallels exist, as among the Eskimos, the Red Indians and the Australian aborigines, there has always been some religious motive to account for them.

Among the aborigines, ritual paintings had to be produced in secret, in a special shelter, and destroyed or hidden when the special rite for which they were made was completed. Animal paintings on rocks in Australia and South Africa had to be regularly renewed, so that the species of animal depicted should not die out. We know of many cases where rock carvings of animals were produced by shamans, in order to help the hunt⁄ers, and to ensure continued fertility among the animals they chose to depict.

The most significant feature of the Scandinavian carvings is their placing. Only a few are found in caves, like the palae⁄olithic examples; the majority are in the open, in inaccessible places unsuitable for habitation. Many are on vertical rock faces or horizontal stones, and nearly all are close to river, lake or sea. They are often found in places still associated with hunting, like the figures of elk carved on flat rocks near the river Etnar at Møllefossan in southern Norway, which are on an ancient track still used by the animals when they come down to cross the river. Sometimes the carvings are so hard to reach that it is presumed that the artists worked from a boat or from some kind of primitive scaffolding. At Sagelva two reindeer are carved on a steep rock wall above a river, so that it is neces⁄sary to be let down on a rope to photograph them, while at Fykanvatn, at the head of a fiord where the waterfall has been harnessed for electric power, figures of reindeer, elk and fish have been deeply cut in the rock on the very edge of the glacier. Some carvings are in the middle of great rivers, and one at Abosjön is 30 metres out from the shore. Others again are near steep cliffs over which in former times hunters are known to have driven the deer, so that animals not killed by the fall could be dispatched by men in boats below. This method of hunting was still practised at Vingen in the eighteenth century, and this area is especially rich in carvings. It has been noted that most of the animals in such sites are facing the water, and sometimes

Plate 2

elk and deer are shown in a wild gallop. Buffalo were killed in this way in North America, and certain myths, like those of the Blackfoot Indians about the Great Bull, who taught a song and dance to a chosen hero to induce the herd to move over the cliff, are associated with such practices. It is not unreasonable to suppose that similar spells and mysteries were once taught to young men in the neighbourhood of the impressive animal figures on the rocky precipices of Norway.

When Father Wilhelm Schmidt in his monumental work, *Der Ursprung der Gottesidee*, outlined the beginnings of religion, he defined the first stage of human society as one of small groups of individuals, perhaps twenty to thirty in size, living a nomad-ic life and depending mostly on hunting, as the Bushmen still do. At this stage there would be equality between the sexes, and boys and girls would be initiated together into crafts and rituals. The attitude of the Bushmen towards the superb animal paintings still surviving in their part of Africa offers a clue to the significance of the early carvings to such little groups of wandering hunters, always remembering that the Bushmen are a small minority surviving in abnormal conditions, and in a very different climate from that of Scandinavia in the Neo-lithic period. The Bushmen looked on the caves and hilltops where the paintings were found as secret sanctuaries, so impor-tant in their community life that in choosing a hunting ground they would search for a site where a rock face was available for painting. In the caves in the blue rock at the Matepos near Bulawayo, the painted animals were thought to represent the herds of the sky against their blue background. Other paint-ings were placed so as to catch the light of morning sun or rising moon. There were also pictures kept for a limited time only and then erased. Frobenius watched a pygmy artist draw-ing an antelope on the ground before he went hunting; a woman with him spoke an incantation, and as the light of the rising sun touched the picture, the hunter transfixed it with an arrow. After the hunt had proved successful and an antelope was killed, the hunter laid blood and hair from the slain animal on his picture, and then erased it as the light of the rising sun reached it on the following morning; Frobenius was told that this was essential if the antelope was not to be 'destroyed'.

Primitive African hunters viewed the sun as the Great Huntsman, since his rays scattered the herds of the night sky, the stars. These represented the animals they knew and formed a kind of platonic image of the ideal herd, of which the creatures on earth were individual examples. The Great Spirit, symbolized by a familiar insect, the praying mantis, protected the creatures to which he had given life. By the right ritual, a slain animal could be raised to rejoin the herds in the sky and later be reborn on earth, and the paintings had to be constantly renewed, so that the heavenly herd stayed intact. The early hunters seem to have had the conception of a limited number of animal and human 'souls', and it is possible that the carvings and paintings provided a resting-place for the wandering spirit until it could enter a new body or journey to the sky. There might also be complex nature symbolism in the paintings, for some of the African animals represented the sun, moon and lightning. To portray the curved horns of the eland could cause the moon to rise from the lake of death, while a springbok drawn inside an elephant meant that lightning was swallowed by a rain-cloud.

It is thus fairly certain that the animal pictures of the Neolithic period were more than accurate records of game made by the hunters. There is no evidence to indicate that they were the totems of different clans, nor does it seem likely that they are examples of crude sympathetic magic, for there are no signs of weapons striking the animals; on the contrary, they are full of vigorous life. Frobenius' evidence suggests that temporary drawings might be transfixed with weapons, and then erased again, while the grand and well-nigh permanent memorials of the wild creatures were for a different purpose, to ensure the continuation of the eternal herds by means of ritual and myth now unknown. It is possible too that the creator spirit and the powers of nature were symbolized in animal form. The creatures in the realistic carvings, the bear, elk, stag and reindeer, might be venerated and loved even though slain for food, and these animals continued to play an important part in religious symbolism long after the close of the Neolithic period.

THE BEGINNINGS OF SHAMANISM

According to Schmidt, the second stage of religious development was that of organized ceremonial in larger communities. At this stage ritual would no longer be practised by members of every family, but by a semi-professional class, the shaman and his disciples. The shaman worked as magician rather than priest, but had to be singled out by special gifts and long training and much silent meditation, in order to act as intermediary between man and the supernatural powers. He could send out his spirit in a trance to discover what was hidden, to heal the sick, to enter the Land of the Dead and return to men, to combat evil powers and to assuage the wrath of the spirits. One of the outstanding characteristics of the shaman everywhere is his close relationship with the animal world, emphasized in costume and ritual, and by the belief in animal spirits helping and hindering him in his endeavours.

From analogies among the hunting peoples of Northern Europe, Asia and North America, it seems reasonable to suppose that shamanism was established among the Scandinavian hunters early in the Neolithic period. The second type of rock pictures, with stylization and esoteric symbolism, strongly suggests shamanistic influence. The 'life-lines' running up to the animals' mouths are found also in the work of Red Indians and the Finno-Ugric peoples, and are known to be the work of shaman artists. The line represents the vital force within the animal, which in death or in a state of trance passes out of the body. The elaborate divisions suggest an interest in anatomy such as frequently forms part of shamanistic lore; it may also be bound up with hunting ritual, and may be compared with the fixed rules for dividing up a slain beast observed in medieval times. Hagen suggests that some of the strange pictures on the rocks might represent the dead animal on its stretched-out skin. Certainly pictures of this type imply complex theories and the acquisition of secret knowledge.

Fig. 3

Human figures which occasionally appear could be the shamans themselves or the spirits with whom they came into contact, taking human as well as animal form. Such figures are seldom drawn realistically, although the human figure was surely not outside the range of such skilled artists, as is proved by a little group scratched on an aurochs bone from Ryemark-gård, Zealand, thought to date from the Mesolithic period. I think it unlikely that these form members of any human family, but that the strange yet effective method chosen to depict them

Fig. 4

Fig. 3   Diagram on rock at Ausevik, Norway (After Hagen)

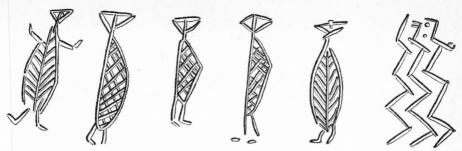

Fig. 4   Figures carved on bone from Ryemarkgård, Zealand, Denmark, about 2.6 cm. in height. In the National Museum, Copenhagen

means that they are members of the spirit world, while the figure on the right suggests a dancing shaman. Another which might show the shaman in his trance is cut on a piece of deer horn from Jordløse Bog, Denmark. There are also naked and hooded figures from Norway, and one of a man in a horned headdress, who is travelling on skis, carved on a cliff at Rødøy, could well represent a shaman on a supernatural journey.

Plate 6

Plate 5

At Solsem there is a rare example of dancing phallic figures painted inside a cave, and the remains of animal and human bones found there, together with fishing and hunting gear, suggest that this may have been a cult sanctuary. It is likely however that such figures belong to the art of a farming community, and not to the hunters. The sacred figures of the hunting people of the North were consistently executed in the open air, in sites close to water and familiar to the hunter, not in enclosed sanctuaries set apart for ritual practices.

RELIGIOUS SYMBOLISM

There is no doubt that the use of symbols was well developed in the Neolithic period. Beside the diagrammatic animals, various abstract symbols are used. 'Frame' symbols are frequent, and these might represent trapping pits, some kind of magic enclosure within which the animal's spirit could be captured, or again symbols of spiritual power. Gjessing notes that they are found near the genitalia of both animals and humans, and that in one case a frame has been placed over the tail of a whale, fraught with special menace for hunters in small boats. Comparison may be made with the Australian *tjurunga*, symbols of magical potency.

Plate 4

In the period of Maglemose culture, men could already produce geometrical and abstract patterns built up from lines, dots, curves and circles. They are unlikely to have been purely decorative, and were presumably meant to add to the efficiency of weapon or tool, or to defend against hostile powers. Animal and human figures are sometimes depicted on bone and horn weapons, and boat symbols are found very early, as can be seen from a hanging ornament from Klepp in Norway with zigzag lines suggesting water. Boats, probably skin canoes, also appear on the rock-carvings, and at Forselv, in a confused mass of figures, a fish is shown hanging from a line fastened to a boat. One boat from Evenhus has three concentric circles on it, and a sun symbol has been suggested for this. It is, however, very hard to date individual cases of this kind. For instance a sun-wheel cut in grooves like the early animal figures at Leiknes in Tysfjord must be post-Neolithic, for it is carved on a rock which was under the sea in the Neolithic period; this serves to remind us that early techniques may have been deliberately copied by later artists. One would expect to find the sun and moon playing an important part in hunting symbolism, but as yet there is no clear evidence for this.

Plate 6

Fertility symbols have been claimed, but are so vague and indeterminate that we need more evidence before accepting them. Although boat and fish symbols might stand for the fertilising power of water, the main impression is that it was the power to maintain the existing stock of living animals rather than the union between male and female which was emphasized, and this is confirmed by evidence from other hunting peoples.

Symbols for rain, lightning and wind might be expected, and the comb-like figure frequent in the more complex carvings could stand for rain. This occurs on bone and amber objects of late Neolithic times in Denmark, and one explanation is that it represents fringes on clothing, but it seems unlikely that this would be so often and carefully depicted. There are also criss-cross lines on weapons and on early Venus figurines from further east, which might be symbols of power. Until we have further evidence, it is hardly profitable to seek to interpret these abstract signs, but it is worth noticing that certain shapes, in particular spiral, triangle, circle and maze, are found at a very early stage.

The development from naturalistic pictures of animals in a vigorous, confident style to cruder, schematic figures and abstract symbols implying knowledge of an esoteric kind is a significant one. The obscure pictures are not aesthetically satisfying, because they have become the means of communication within a restricted group. As Kuhn points out in his description of the Spanish rock paintings, this is the point at which an alphabet might develop, if an organized, leisured priesthood were available to work on it. But there was no such body of men in Scandinavia, and instead of developing further the symbols were to change drastically in style and content.

THE CARE OF THE DEAD

We have seen that evidence from the hunting culture in early Scandinavia implies a sense of affinity between men and animals, growth of religious symbolism, and a shamanistic form of religion, based on the idea of a life spirit which leaves the body. Of the other two behaviour patterns mentioned at the outset, there is little direct evidence. We have reason to believe that offerings were made, and that these were associated with the powerful animals carved on the rocks. There is implication also that early man here as elsewhere felt no permanent gulf be- tween the worlds of living and dead, and that belief in the rebirth of slaughtered wild creatures – and by analogy, of hu- man beings – formed part of his early religious beliefs. If there was a belief in the release of the spirit, as the symbolism of the more complex carvings suggests, this could encourage a belief in a land of the dead to which the spirit might journey, and from which it might return to the world of men. But such a belief leaves no clear trace on archaeological remains in Scan- dinavia, and as yet no elaborate graves from the Mesolithic or Early Neolithic periods have been found.

In Denmark a grave from the Kongemose culture at Ved- bæk was found in 1944 under an undisturbed pile of rubbish on a dwelling site. The dead man lay on his back under four large stones, without grave goods. He may even have been placed there before the arrival of the Kongemose folk. Another grave at Korsøv Nor was on sloping ground near the dwel- lings, where the dead man lay on a sheet of bark, with another placed over him, and with a flint tool at his side. The men of the Ertebølle or Kitchen Midden culture buried their dead with care in simple graves inside the heaps of shells and bones marking their dwelling sites along the shore. A hunter from Bäskaskog, Kiaby, in Sweden was found in a sitting position in an oval grave, with his fishing spear and knife. All this shows that the dead were interred with respect and care, but with no special rites or indication of belief in a future state. For new emphasis on the resting place of the dead, we must await the coming of the new crafts of tilling the soil and harvesting the crops.

CHAPTER II

The Sacred Tomb

In life one house, in death one grave.

MALAGASY PROVERB

THE FARMING COMMUNITY

IN THE THIRD MILLENNIUM before Christ a new way of life reached Denmark from the south, and was adopted by many of the hunting and fishing communities there. For the first time they learned simple farming, and began to herd animals and to grow crops in village communities, clearing the forests by burning in order to cultivate barley and a primitive kind of wheat. We know that this way of life was practised in Muldbjorg in west Zealand by about 2600 BC, and the burning of the forests has left traces in the Danish bogs. New ideas of this kind must have been welcomed in Denmark, where it was now becoming difficult to find animals to hunt, for fish and fruit could not have been a wholly satisfying diet. In a century or so agriculture spread to south Sweden and from there to eastern Norway. It appears that in all regions animal farming and agriculture came in about the same time.

There were three significant characteristics of the new farming communities. Men now lived in settled village groups; they discovered the importance of domesticated animals, and in particular of cattle, sheep and pigs. Moreover, they practised a new skill, the laying of seed deliberately in the earth in order to obtain the life-giving grain. This far-reaching change in the way of living was reflected inevitably in their religion.

Whenever agriculture is introduced into the lives of hunting peoples, the practice of making sacrifices of living creatures, both animals and men, takes on a new importance. In many parts of the world a myth develops about a divine man, woman or animal, who perished in order to bring the gift of edible plants to man. Once men settle in a community and cease to lead a nomadic life, the abiding place of the dead comes to be viewed as a source of power, and this, rather than the remote sanctuary or holy place, becomes the centre of religious cults. The collective rites of the community take on a new pattern, and are associated with ploughing, seed⁄time and harvest, the key points of the farmer's year, while the priest, rather than the shaman, becomes the guardian of the new mysteries. Mytholog⁄ical concepts which emerge are those of the all⁄powerful goddess who makes the earth fruitful, the great serpent bringing wisdom and new foods, the labyrinth of death, and the door to the Other World. This is the background against which we can place evidence from the Late Neolithic period in Scandinavia.

THE STONE SEPULCHRE

For the first time in Scandinavia the tomb became important in the life of the community. The stone⁄built grave known as the dolmen (Danish *dysse,* Swedish *dös*) was established in Den⁄mark in the third millennium BC, although the origin and history of this form of tomb in the North is a very complex question. The megalithic tomb, built of great blocks of stone, appeared in the Mediterranean area during the fourth millen⁄nium, and gradually spread over most of Western Europe, with considerable variation of plan and structure in different areas. According to the traditional theory, the earliest Scandina⁄vian examples are single chamber graves, dated by Becker to period C of the Neolithic; these are simple rectangular enclo⁄sures built of large flat boulders, with a great cover⁄stone on top. These are plentiful in Denmark, where such stones are easily available, and to a less extent in south Sweden. The building technique implies considerable experience, for it could not have been easy, even with the use of rollers and ramps of earth, to place such huge stones in position. The chambers are mostly

Plate 8

raised above ground, and covered by an earth mound about 6 Plate 7
feet high, with a ring of stones forming a kerb around the base.

Dating of such tombs is very difficult, and previous theories will probably have to be revised on account of new Carbon 14 dates from Neolithic contexts, which push the establishment of great stone tombs in Northern Europe much further back than has been previously assumed. Nearly all these graves have been emptied of grave goods long ago, and it is thus not easy to determine which type is the earliest in Denmark. There is not even agreement as to whether the earliest stone tombs were introduced by invaders from abroad. The tendency now is to argue that they began independently in the North, developing out of simple rectangular or round graves in the earth, lined with stones, such as continued to be used by some of the peo/ ples living in Denmark in the late Neolithic period.

Without entering into the complicated arguments about the origin of megalithic tombs in Denmark, there are two points of significance for the religious historian. First, it was now thought important to produce permanent and impressive memorials for the dead, and men were willing to undertake organized labour to achieve this. Secondly, this new type of grave, whatever its immediate origin, fits into the general pattern of stone burial chambers erected in many parts of Western Europe. The fact that in Scandinavia also men turned to follow this prevailing fashion must have been due to their religious concepts about the dead.

Some communities, like the people of the Battle/Axe cul/ ture, which begins in Denmark roughly half/way through the Neolithic period (about BC 2000) continued to bury their dead in single graves in the earth. But the dolmens proved so popular that over 2000 of them survive in Zealand alone. These are stone graves built to endure, and stand above ground, a visible symbol of the dwelling of the dead. While the characteristic dolmen has no entrance, some are provided with a kind of

Plate 8

door, when one short side is built lower than the rest. In Bohus-län and Scania a triangular opening is made by bringing two wall-stones together at the top and setting a threshold stone below, emphasizing the resemblance to a house. Some graves have a rudimentary passage, formed by two stones placed at the entry to the chamber. It is thought that many of these graves were not wholly covered by earth, but that the cover-stone remained visible on top of the mound. Thus the home of the dead was not presented as a house permanently shut and barred.

There is considerable variation in the structure of the stone chambers, which may be rectangular, polygonal or round, and the distribution of the various types does not easily fit into any theory of chronological development. Sometimes there are two or more chambers within a long mound, and this may have led towards the building of a large family grave. The dolmens do not seem to have held many burials, or to have been intend-ed to serve as communal graves. Once the great megalithic passage graves developed, however, the idea of a house for the lonely dead was abandoned in favour of a grave which would hold large numbers.

It may not be a coincidence that at about the time when elab-orate stone-built graves were developing in Denmark, we have also evidence for the earliest village communities, like Barkær in Djursland. This site, on a peninsula jutting out into a lake, consisted of two rectangular houses divided into rooms, large enough to hold several families. They were in fact 'long houses', in which related families could live and work together. It would hardly be surprising if a community of this kind came to construct graves which were imitations of their earthly dwellings, and it would be natural for them to welcome a reli-gion emphasizing the significance of the dead in the grave, and the potency of departed ancestors to bring blessing to the community. The centre for rites to placate the dead would naturally be where members of the community were buried.

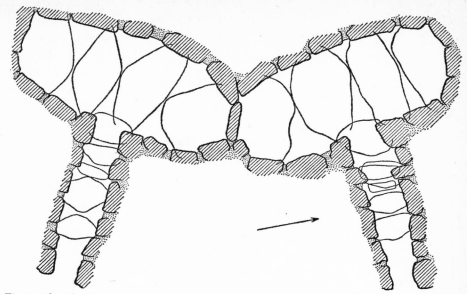

Fig. 5   Plan of twin passage graves in Troldhøj, Odsherred, Denmark (after Brøndsted)

The great passage graves which mark the climax of megalithic culture in the North consist of chambers built of enormous blocks of stone with a passage of considerable length leading in to them. Sometimes a pair of such graves was built symmetrically, as at Troldhøj, Odsherred, in Denmark. It seems that the passage remained open until the grave was felt to be full, and it was then sealed, and a mound of earth heaped over the stones. These graves were certainly used for many generations as resting-places for the dead, forming the centre of ceremonies which must have been regular, solemn and impressive. At Luttra in Sweden, for instance, and Hyldehøj, Kalundborg, in Denmark, as many as a hundred individuals were buried in one grave.

Plates 9, 10

Fig. 5

33

There is no means of telling whether the bodies were placed in the chamber immediately after death, or whether they were kept elsewhere until the flesh had disappeared from the bones. In some graves bones have been found in confusion, but this might be caused by earlier interments being disturbed to make way for later ones. However, the passages were in many cases so low and narrow that they would need to be entered by men crawling on hands and knees, and it would be difficult to take in a dead body unless the passage were left unroofed during the time that the grave was in use.

The two points of entry were the stone threshold of the chamber, where wooden doors were probably provided, and the opening into the passage from outside. This opening was sometimes emphasized by a wall of stones built on either side, curved to form a kind of forecourt, and at this point enormous quantities of pottery and animal bones have been found, implying sacrificial meals or offerings to the dead. One large passage grave at Gronhøj in east Jutland produced as many as 7,000 potsherds and a number of upturned pots, and when the sherds were pieced together it was evident that rows of pots had stood either on the stones forming the forecourt, or just behind them.

At Tustrup near Aarhus a stone building of some size had been built beside a passage grave, with one wall left open. It had no hearth, but the remains of bowls and ladles were found inside, some richly decorated, and there was an oval hollow in the floor. The building was burnt down not long after it was built, and it may have been a temporary resting-place for the body until the bones were ready for the grave.

In a study published early in this century, the anthropologist Robert Hertz collected evidence which has some bearing on this problem. He shows that over a surprisingly large part of the world, and especially in agricultural communities, it has been customary to hold a second funeral ceremony after the

decay of the body. The aim is to purify the dead by the removal
of the perishable parts, and both cremation and embalment
might indeed be viewed as developments from this. At the
final rites there is always much feasting and rejoicing, accompanied by sacrifices and ceremonies of purification, while the
cleansed bones are placed in a permanent sepulchre, sometimes
shared by the whole village community. The spirit of the dead
is then deemed to be free to enter the spirit world, while the
living are safe from the dangers that threatened while the decay-
ing body rested in their midst. Examples given by Hertz from
Indonesia, the Pacific Islands and America are significant in
the light of archaeological evidence from the passage graves. In
particular the widespread custom of collecting liquids from the
body during the period of transition (to be disposed of in
various ways repulsive to a modern mind), and the subsequent
shattering of the vessels which had contained them, might
serve as a clue to explain the breaking of so much pottery in the
vicinity of the passage graves. It also reminds us that pots
could be used for other purposes than that of holding food and
drink or libations to the dead.

A part from the pots and bowls, there is little direct evidence
for ritual; carved stones such as are found in megalithic tombs
in Brittany and the British Isles are absent. One motif associated with such tombs is the face with staring eyes, sometimes
forming part of a stylized female figure with bare breasts and
a necklace. This is assumed to represent the great Mother
Goddess, a chthonic deity of the Neolithic period associated
with fertility and the dead. The carvings must be linked with
the so-called Venus figurines in bone, stone and mammoth
ivory which appear in the Palaeolithic period among the
mammoth hunters of Eastern Europe. These are naked female
figures with a featureless face, feeble arms and legs, tiny or non-
existent feet, and all the emphasis placed on huge breasts, hips,
loins and abdomen. They are found in sacred caves and house

sites, and there is little doubt that their main purpose was a protective one, defending hearth and home, children, crops and cattle from danger and disease. This protective goddess took on new importance in the period of the first planters, when women became the guardians of the food-giving seed, and it was among farming communities that belief in a female goddess of plenty developed. It has been suggested that the great megalithic tomb-temples of Malta were themselves a symbolic rendering of the rounded female form.

In Scandinavia, however, we lack the early Venus figurines, and there is no symbolic carving on the tombs to make their meaning clearer. There is reason to believe that the worship of the goddess of death and fruitfulness prevailed here, as elsewhere among the megalithic builders, but it was evidently not customary to depict her in visible form in stone. The staring eyes are

Fig. 6

occasionally found on pots in Denmark, but such vessels are relatively rare, and it has been thought by some that they are 'face urns' intended to represent the dead. There is no sign of the maze, a motif which Knight claimed to recognize in the cairn of Bryn Celli Ddu in Anglesey and which he believed represented the difficult passage to the spirit world. We have only the ring of kerbstones which consistently encircles the house of the dead; this might be seen as a stone necklace on the bosom of the earth, or, like the maze, a symbol of the barrier shutting in the dangerous world of the dead. However, it is possible to see in the tombs with their narrow opening and rounded or square stone chamber the image of the dark, sheltering womb of Mother Earth, while the triangular openings and curving 'horns' of the forecourts could also be viewed as female symbols of the goddess. The idea that the dead rest in the womb, awaiting rebirth after a sojourn with the ancestors, is a belief commonly associated with the practice of collective burial, and ceremonies at the threshold may well have emphasized the freeing of the spirit for its next adventure.

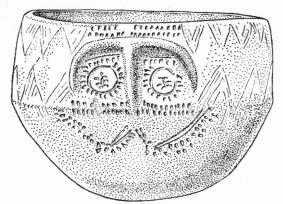

Fig. 6 Face urn from east Denmark, Late Neolithic, about 11 cm. in height. In the National Museum, Copenhagen

The builders of these tombs had grown familiar with the idea of an apparently dead seed laid in the earth springing forth to new life after the winter darkness. The imaginative and symbolic possibilities of this discovery were limitless, finding expression in new myths and ritual everywhere. Thus for the first time the laying of the dead within the earth became directly associated with a belief in some kind of rebirth. Since those who lived together in the earthly community were laid together in the sacred spot, this would give rise to more elaborate beliefs in a land of the dead to which the living might obtain entry, and from which the dead might return to visit them. The collective burials in the passage graves imply a cult of ancestors, emphasizing the importance of family and clan, and the link between the living and the dead.

FAMILY GRAVES

Not all shared the religion of the builders of the megalithic graves. The people of the Pitted-Ware culture, for instance, who settled round the Scandinavian coasts in the Middle Neolithic period, continued to bury their dead on the dwelling site, together with tools, weapons and ornaments, but these were not true farming people, since they lived largely by fishing and herding. The Battle-Axe people, who settled in Denmark about the same time, were for their part a semi-nomadic and pastoral folk, keeping herds in the plains and along the river-sides, and they preferred to bury their dead in low mounds. Sometimes one grave was set above another, so that the mound gradually grew higher, or occasionally they made use of exist-ing passage graves. By the close of the Neolithic period, these people with different funerary practices seem to have settled down to a fairly stable existence side by side. By the time that copper and bronze weapons were coming into use in the North, communal graves were being built once more.

This may have been due to the fact that more people were growing crops and living in settled communities, so that it seemed natural to bury several generations in a common tomb. The tombs of the Late Neolithic period were usually below ground, and might consist of a simple stone cist, holding a few bodies, or a huge burial chamber as much as ten yards in length. Once more an opening was left at the side, where a wooden door may have been fitted. In central Sweden the cham-ber might be divided into several rooms, with holes in the partition walls large enough for a man to clamber through. The number of people buried in a tomb varied greatly. One grave at Dragny, near Uppsala, held twenty, but a small grave in Västergotland had at least sixty. Similar graves with holed partitions used for massed burials have been found in northern France, and these again have stylized carvings of the female form, lacking in the Scandinavian examples.

Clearly the cult of collective burial in a stone tomb went on for many centuries, for there are more than 4,000 megalithic graves in Denmark and some hundreds in southern Sweden. Some passage graves and stone cists were used up to the end of the Neolithic period, and the pattern is so firmly defined that it

Plate 11

implies fixed ritual continuing over the centuries. One purpose of the rites at the tomb must have been to ensure the continuing fertility of the soil, characteristic of the farmers as opposed to the nomadic hunters. Their dead were firmly enclosed in the earth, surrounded by great stones and imprisoned in a circle of potency, and venerated in their home precincts, among the fields of their descendants. One would expect to find a priest presiding over the organized ceremonies and seasonal festivals, established in the atmosphere of faithful conservatism which distinguishes a flourishing priesthood and differs fundamentally from the more individual and imaginative ritual of the shaman. It was probably the priest who passed through the doors of the dead, linking up the dark tomb-world with the living, and bearing purified bones inside to lie beside those of the ancestors. He would no doubt conduct sacrificial rites, in which plants, animals and humans were offered up to the powers which ruled the underworld. But here the archaeological evidence fails us, and we can only surmise the rites from what is known of later cults associated with the Great Goddess.

VOTIVE OFFERINGS

Throughout the later Neolithic period, isolated objects and small hoards were left in the part of Denmark now covered by peat. The ground may not then have been marshy, and in some cases is known to have been forest land, or under water. In the period extending from about 2500 to 2000 BC, the objects deposited were mainly flint axes, stone clubs, amber beads, and small clay pots.

When we find a set of fine flint axes in mint condition, or sets of mixed daggers and chisels in flint and bone, these may well have been hidden by traders or craftsmen who meant to recover them; single objects may have been accidentally lost. But there are many finds not associated with grave or dwelling place which seem to be votive offerings. In 1927 Bjorn counted as many as 48 of these from Norway alone, and the numbers over the Scandinavian area have grown steadily since then.

Tools and weapons must have been of enormous importance to early man, offering supremacy over the animal world and a chance of survival, so that they would naturally be viewed as symbols of power. The most valuable was the axe, used in Denmark from the Mesolithic period onwards, since it enabled the early farmers to clear the land for crops. Axes have been found in the bogs carefully placed in pairs, standing on edge. In a house site at Troldbjerg in Denmark of late Neolithic date, a polished stone axe with edge turned upward and a small clay pot were found in a shallow hole in the floor, clear evidence for the sanctity of the axe as an object of power. Small greenstone axes with the necks pierced for suspension have also been found, presumably worn as amulets.

The type of axe found in the bogs is usually the working tool of the farmer, and it is seldom new, appearing often to be of earlier date than other objects found with it. Possibly a few unfinished or unused specimens found were specially made for the offering, but we have no way of telling.

Clay pots are thought to have held food – perhaps butter or animal fat – and to have been women's offerings. They are also found in graves, as at Volling, Salling, where twelve finely decorated little pots lay along one side. Amber beads, worn by both men and women, are also found in graves, and at one at Salten in Sanderborg there were about a hundred strewn over the body, while flint axes, arrowheads, and a broken disc of sheet copper had been placed by the dead.

At Åmosen in western Zealand a number of dug-out canoes were preserved in the peat, and some appear to have been deliberate offerings. Remains of a clay hearth were found inside two of the boats, with animal bones and potsherds, while in front of one was an almost complete human skeleton. Some of the boats were anchored by stones and others appear to have been surrounded by a fence.

The practice of votive offerings was to continue long after the Neolithic period, and there must have been many established holy places where humble offerings were made to the powers in remote spots. The farmers' axes, pots of food and amber beads would all be in keeping with a cult of the goddess among people who tilled the ground, and such offerings are also associated with the dead. Whether the emphasis on the axe implies a thunder god associated with the goddess as her husband (see p. 53) at this early period it is not yet possible to say. Certainly we have ample evidence for simple solemnities forming part of man's everyday religion, to set beside the more elaborate ceremonial of the great family graves.

CHAPTER III
The Advent of the Gods

The two hills are divided; the god comes into being.

PYRAMID TEXTS

NEW FUNERAL CUSTOMS

ALTHOUGH NO ABRUPT change in culture and religious practice is indicated between the Late Neolithic and the early Bronze Age, we very soon find ourselves in a new climate of thought. Metal came gradually into use for tools and weapons, and the Bronze Age in Scandinavia is held to have lasted roughly a thousand years, from about 1600 to 450 BC. In this period great progress was made in social organisation, art and craftsmanship, and new religious ideas of considerable potency were adopted in the North. Some of the inspiration behind these may have come from Central Europe and ultimately from the Near East; others may have been already present in Denmark in the Neolithic period. The effect on ritual and symbolism is far-reaching, as may be seen from funeral customs, cult objects, and above all from the rock carvings of Sweden and southern Norway, where those practising new rites have left a vivid picture of their activities.

The break with the religion of the megalithic builders is clearly shown by the change in funeral customs. Already in the Late Neolithic period the Battle-Axe people had prepared single graves for their distinguished dead. These folk seem to have been warriors, living in a heroic age, to judge from the fine weapons laid with them in the grave and sometimes found in hoards. Their custom of burial in a stone cist within a mound went on into the Early Bronze Age. Sometimes secondary burials were made in the mounds, but they were essentially single graves of chieftains, not family sepulchres. As Scandinavia grew more prosperous, fine objects of native craftsmanship were placed in the graves, and larger mounds were built for the dead. These graves stood in high places, where they would be landmarks for travellers, and sometimes in a row along the ancient trackways. While the megalithic tomb served as the enduring home of the gathered dead, the single barrow or cairn commemorated the famous hero who would be long remembered. Both were undoubtedly places of sanctity and power.

Sometimes the dead lay in a cist below a cairn of stones under an earth mound. A ring of stones surrounded the mound, as in the earlier period, but these were usually smaller than the boulders of the megalithic graves, and were sometimes built into a dry-stone wall, covered by the mound. Outside the mound, traces of enclosures often survive, where ceremonies may have taken place. Ploughing probably formed part of the rites, since marks of ploughshares have been found under a number of Danish barrows. The scattering of charcoal while the barrow was being built, and the trampling of areas round the grave by marching or dancing feet, were other possibilities suggested by Sir Cyril Fox, from the evidence of Bronze Age mounds excavated in South Wales. He also found traces of boughs laid over the ground at burial, and sheaves of wheat and barley in a pit, as well as evidence for the kindling of fires.

Scattered evidence from many Bronze Age sites implies elaborate and varied ritual accompanying the building of the mounds, and the hallowing of the ground before and during the funeral. There are many flat-topped howes in Jutland, one at Nustrup, Haderslev, being over 67 metres long and about 2 metres high. These, according to Brøndsted, are popularly known as *Dansehøje*, Dance howes, and the modern name may reflect a genuine ancient tradition. They would be well fitted for use as platforms if ceremonies were held over the grave.

While there must have been many local divergencies in funeral rites, three important innovations can be clearly discerned:

the use of tree coffins for the dead, the building of a symbolic house of the dead within the mound, and the burning of the body.

Coffins made from trunks of large oak-trees came in during the Early Bronze Age and were much used on the Danish mainland. In some cases tannin in the wood has preserved the coffin and its contents, and cloth, grave goods and even the hair of the dead have survived. The tree was carefully hollowed out, and the body laid inside one section on a cowhide, some-

Plate 12

times resting on a layer of grass and flowers. Excavation of tightly-sealed oak coffins from Skrydstrup, Borum Æshøj, Egtved and Trindhøj have taught us much about the appear-ance of Bronze Age folk, since both men and women were buried fully clothed, equipped with weapons and ornaments. Drink was supplied in a wooden vessel or birch-bark pail, and occasional luxuries, such as a folding stool from Guldhøj, left with the dead. Oak coffins from the Middle Bronze Age have also been excavated in southern Sweden, and at Eldsberga, south Halland, a man and woman in two coffins were found inside one mound.

In similar graves from the British Isles, dug-out boats seem sometimes to have been used for coffins, at as Eylston and Loose Howe in Yorkshire. A canoe from a dried-up lake in Sweden closely resembles the tree coffins, so that some Scandinavian examples may also have been boats or imitations of boats. Such elaborate repositories needing so much labour to produce must surely have had a symbolic significance, for the stone cist al-ready provided a lasting container for the dead. The coffin had a lid in imitation of the cist, but its likeness to a boat is borne out by other symbolism of the period. In particular it is con-firmed by the outline of a boat made with stones round many graves in the Late Bronze Age in eastern Sweden and the Danish islands. In Gotland alone there are more than 300 of

Plate 14

these 'ship-settings', which form beautiful and impressive memorials. The ship is outlined in large upright stones, with a transverse slab for the stern and one narrow boulder for the prow, and can be of great size; one at Gannarve is about 50 yards in length. It is not certain how many of these stone ships are built over graves, as few have been carefully excavated. A ship under a mound at Lugnare, south Halland, had a cremation burial in an urn wrapped in cloth by its side, undoubtedly contemporary with it. The ships left above ground may have had some ritual part to play, and at Litsemose, Tullebølle, there was a circle cut in a stone at the prow, which gave rise to the suggestion that it had represented the ship of the sun.

The practice of building a house over the dead seems at first sight to contradict the symbol of a boat. Fox found remains of simple buildings in South Wales, one at Llantwit Major formed of stakes and wattle-work with a roof supported by a central ring of posts, and another at Six Wells apparently consisting of a low wall only and no roof. 'Death-houses' are rare in Denmark, but have been found in Thuringia, some way south of the border, and there are a few traces in carefully excavated Danish barrows. At Grunhof-Tesperude, Lauenburg, just beyond the border, a long oblong howe held two coffins, with cremated remains of a woman and a child. These lay in a square marked out with postholes, and covered with stones; it seemed that a house with one open side had been built to hold them, and then burned with the coffins and bodies, after which the mound was raised over the pyre. Thus the erection of a house could form part of the ritual in cremation as well as inhumation burials. A small turfed building stood beside a grave of the Early Bronze Age at Jægerspris, and traces of others covered by mounds have been found in Sweden, indicating that a ritual house may have been erected for the funeral celebrations.

A number of cremation urns from south Sweden, Gotland and Denmark have been made in the shape of a round hut, with a square door in the side. Sometimes this door forms the

Plate 13

Plate 22

opening, and has a lid to fit it, or there may be an opening in the roof where the smoke-hole would be. The urn from Stora Hammar in Scania has been boldly painted in black and yellow, so that the resemblance to a circular hut with thatched roof, side entrance, and other doors or openings around the walls is quite clear. This is unlikely to be the model of an ordinary dwelling-house, but rather of a 'death-house' in which the body was placed. The idea of house-urns came from the south, and they are known in north Germany, Pomerania and Italy, but the fact that such a custom was adopted in Scandinavia was probably due to familiarity with the idea of a house for the dead. Such a house would be a temporary one, intended to hold the body until the time for purification was over, and it continued to be built on the funeral pyre for many centuries.

The change from inhumation to cremation in the Bronze Age was a radical one, yet it came about slowly and gradually, and does not appear to be due to startling new beliefs about the dead. It began about the middle of the Bronze Age, and by the close of the period was almost universal in Scandinavia. There are instances of burnt grave goods from the Neolithic period, and one cremation grave was found at Stenildgaard near Aars, but this is clearly exceptional, and perhaps a foreigner's grave. Fires, however, formed part of the ritual in or near the tomb long before cremation was adopted. The Single Grave people sometimes lit one in the grave, and in one Norwegian burial of the Boat-Axe people excavated in 1942 small grave goods and bones were found on a layer of cinders at the bottom of the grave.

Once cremation became general, there was plenty of variation in the treatment of the burnt bones, which might be placed in clay urns, containers of wood, bark or metal, or in little stone cists. Sometimes full-length cists were built as if for a burial, and the bones spread out in a thin layer over the whole grave, as at Ørnehøj, Bønnerup, or even laid out with clothing spread over them, as at Lyngby, northern Jutland. Grave goods were usually laid unburnt beside the ashes, except for ornaments worn by the dead. Sometimes tree-coffins were used, or the burnt remains put into a small grave in an existing burial mound. At Egtved the cremated remains of a child accompa- nied a woman buried unburnt in a tree coffin, and some of the Welsh mounds excavated by Fox held cremated remains of children as well as the main inhumation burial. He has sug- gested that these might be examples of human sacrifice, to sanctify the site or accompany the high-born dead, but possibly in a transition stage young children were cremated and adults buried with more conservative rites.

Plate 12

Since cremation is associated with earlier forms of burial in this way, it would seem that the practice won gradual accept- ance because it harmonized with prevailing religious ideas. We shall see that the rock carvings give evidence for the wor- ship of a sky-god as well as an earth-goddess. The religion of the sky does not necessarily include the practice of cremation, but it is consistent with it, since fire may be seen as the symbol of both the sun and the lightning, two mysterious forces con- nected with the deity of the sky. To worshippers of a sky-god, the practice of cremation must have appeared seemly and con- venient, and the funeral pyre had great dramatic possibilities, rivalling those of the passage grave, for staging the solemn departure of the dead from among the living. Ritual fires were already known, and though there is no clear evidence for sacri- fice by burning, it would be surprising if this played no part in the early farming communities. The cremation burials devel- oped traditional symbolism of their own. Sometimes towards the close of the Bronze Age the wings of birds were placed in the urns with the ashes, and instances of jackdaws, crows and rooks have been recorded from urns in Denmark. Of the possible implications of this, more will be said below (p. 58).

THE KIVIK GRAVE

A link between the funeral practices of the Bronze Age and the rock carvings is afforded by the unique grave of Bredarör, near Kivik in Scania, which contained a series of impressive and mysterious carvings on the eight stones forming the grave chamber. The grave was in a huge mound, 75 metres in diameter, and in 1748 two farmers who had been taking stones from the cairn which covered the grave came upon the capstone of the cist, organised a treasure-hunt by night, and destroyed the site so effectively that nothing is now left but the carvings. The stones themselves were badly damaged, and one was lost long ago, so that we have to rely partly on contemporary drawings.

In spite of its sad history this grave remains one of the most important memorials of the Bronze Age in Europe. The carvings have been compared with the wall-paintings from another outstanding work, the sarcophagus from Hagia Triada in Crete, which is late Minoan work of about 1400 BC. These paintings depict ritual connected with the dead man, who is shown standing before his tomb. Men sacrifice an ox, pour libations, bring offerings, and walk in procession to the music of a flute. While the Swedish carvings differ greatly in style and treatment, there is some resemblance in subject matter.

Fig. 7
Plate 15

On the Bredarör stones numbered 7 and 8 there are processions of men blowing *lurer*, long horns such as we know were used in Scandinavia during the Bronze Age, and others standing by two omega-like shapes, which might be plans of tombs or enclosures of some kind. It has been suggested that they are fertility symbols, representing both the womb and the rounded tomb within the earth with its narrow entrance. There are other processions of either men or women in long robes, whose strange pointed heads suggest bird masks, approaching an altar or cauldron, perhaps for some libation ceremony. On stone 7 a man stands facing a similar procession, his hands upraised in an attitude of worship. Another is driving a two-horse

Fig. 7   Slab no. 8 from Kivik grave, Scania, after restoration. Historiska Museum ,Stock-holm

chariot, and two horses face each other, as if for a horse fight —both pictures suggesting funeral games. A puzzling scene on stone 8 shows two men in a rounded enclosure on either side of an upright pole, holding objects or ropes suspended from it. The most interesting suggestion is that this is a fire-drilling ceremony, the kindling of the sacred flame, but there is nothing to confirm this. A large fish on stone 7 may stand for water or the sea, or represent the funeral meal. In spite of varying inter-pretations, it seems reasonable to suppose that these two stones show rites connected with the funeral, as at Hagia Triada. Both works belong approximately to the same period, although our ignorance of the contents of the Kivik grave makes dating very difficult. There is no reason, however, to assume any direct relationship between them.

The remaining Kivik slabs bear symbols familiar from other sources. The lost stone showed two curved axes, supported as

Fig. 7

Plate 15

Plate 16

though mounted on stands, and below these was a stylized picture of a boat. A cone-shaped object in the centre is obscure. On slab 2 is a ship holding either rowers or a line of discs on poles, as shown in the rock carvings. Slab 3 shows two pairs of horses, one pair facing right, the other face to face, and between the pairs, lines of zig-zag decoration suggesting water. Slab 4 has two similar decorative panels, and in the centre two circles with crosses, possibly wheels or sun-discs. Slab 5 is too poorly preserved to describe, and Slab 6 has two more wheel-discs, and two sylized axes above.

Plate 15

The only way to interpret such scenes and symbols is by detailed comparisons with a large number of figures from various Bronze Age sources, in Scandinavia and further afield. The work done by Sprockhoff on certain ornamental motifs is an excellent example of this method of approach. Here, it is only possible to make some general observations. We have a grave tentatively dated to the Middle Bronze Age, perhaps about 1200 BC, offering us an elaborate body of symbolism connected with the dead. It shows that those who prepared the grave for king or priest must have been members of some organized cult of considerable complexity. The symbols them-selves are not an isolated phenomenon, for although they are not found in other graves of the period, they are to a large ex-tent echoed in the rock carvings, while other interesting paral-lels are found outside Scandinavia, particularly in Minoan religious art. It is necessary, however, to study the rock carvings to see the Kivik symbols against a wider background.

THE ROCK PICTURES

Scenes and symbols of considerable complexity have been carved during the Bronze Age in Scandinavia. Most of these are in western Sweden, between Gothenburg and Oslo Fjord, including a rich collection at Bohuslän, but there is a series from Östergotland, and a third group round Simrishamn in eastern Scania (Skåne), not far from Kivik. Additions are constantly being made to the list, and one series round Enköping in Uppland has not yet been published. There are also isolated carvings on Gotland, Öland and Bornholm, and a number in Denmark. More have been found at Østfold in Norway, in small groups from Lista, Rogaland and further up the coast, and several in Trøndelag. Thus the material is widely scattered.

These carvings differ from the animal carvings of the Stone Age in both style and content. They form a clearly defined group, with a limited series of motifs repeated very frequently. It has been shown convincingly by Oscar Almgren and others that the actions portrayed on the rocks are mainly of ritual significance, concerned with religious ceremonies in which many people take part. Beside scenes of action, there appear many objects of practical use, like ploughs, weapons and boats, and others which seem to be made for a ritual purpose, like the sun-discs. There are human figures of enormous size, which might depict idols or anthropomorphic deities, and representations of human hands and feet; there are also many animals, birds and fish.

These carvings are mainly concerned with agriculture and war. Beside ploughs and wagons and sledges such as the farmers used, domestic animals such as horses, pigs, cattle and goats are clearly recognizable. On the military side, axe, spear, sword and bow are depicted, and there are chariots and ships in large numbers, and scenes of fighting. The dominant part is taken by men, and women appear only rarely.

One very prominent object is a disc-like shape, which may be shown as a plain or a decorated circle, or as a wheel with four or eight spokes. Men raise their hands to this disc in worship, or hold it up, and it is sometimes set on a support or stand, or carried on a ship. There are also men with bodies in

Plate 18

51

Fig. 8 Axe-bearer on rock at Simrislund, Tanum, Bohuslän (after Almgren)

the form of discs, some carrying weapons. This disc must be an object of importance and reverence, and there seems little doubt that it represents the sun. Models of such discs have been found in Denmark, one a small amber disc with a cross cut in it which shows when held up to the light, set on a handle like those shown in the carvings. Even more striking is the famous disc from Trundholm in north-western Zealand, plated with gold and elaborately decorated with circles and spirals; it is set on wheels and drawn by a horse of bronze – probably one of a pair. There is record of a another wagon from Tagaborgshöjden in Sweden with a disc of bronze, said to be as big as a cabbage leaf, from which only the bronze animals which drew it have survived.

Discs on wagons imply a conception of the sun travelling across the heavens, and so does the disc in a boat, which occurs frequently on rocks and metal objects of the Bronze Age. The idea of a boat of the sun can be traced to various parts of the world in antiquity, and was richly developed in Ancient Egypt. Sprockhoff suggests that a separate conception, that of the chariot drawn by swans or ducks, came into Scandinavia from Central Europe, where little models of such chariots have been found. He believes that two separate means of transport were envisaged, a journey across the sky in a chariot by day, and beneath the earth in a boat by night. This might explain the association of boats with the dead. The different ideas could exist side by side, just as varying poetic images for the sun may be found in one poem. The little walking discs might be stylized renderings of warriors with shields, but could possibly be men of the sun, taking part in ritual combats.

The axe plays an important part in the carvings. It is not associated with a goddess, as in Crete, but is generally held by a male figure, who may be of great size. Huge axes are also shown held by tiny men. Sometimes the axe is mounted on a stand, or on a ship, and it is frequently found with the sun-disc. Again we have ritual objects as parallels, in the form of splen- did axes too large to be put to practical use, from Sweden and Denmark, which seem to have been left as votive offerings. One fine example from Västerås weighs 3.5 kilogrammes, and is far too heavy to use, while two from Skogstorp are of thin bronze over a clay core; both are very similar in shape to the axes on the Kivik stone, as are also those forming another pair from Vejle in Jutland. These axes date from the Middle Bronze Age, and from the Late Bronze Age we have little figures of men holding axes, of which more will be said below (see p. 60).

Fig. 8
Plate 18

Plate 19

The history of religion in Europe and the Near East shows that both sun-disc and axe are associated with the god of the sky. The axe in the god's hand is a symbol of the thunderbolt, later to be pictured in Scandinavia as a hammer, and such a symbol probably goes back to the Stone Age, when axes were left as votive offerings. There is a direct connection between the lightning and the sun; the lightning is the fire from heaven, coming down to earth both to preserve and destroy, for, while it slays those who come in its path, it also brings the life-giving rain. The sun also is the beneficial fire from heaven, giving life and causing the seed to grow, while in the North it is the great liberator, breaking through the winter dark. Thus both are connected with the sky and the fruitfulness of the earth. The conception of marriage between the god of the sky and the goddess of earth was familiar among the agricultural peoples of the Near East and the Mediterranean area, and during the Bronze Age this idea seems also to have reached the North.

Certain scenes on the rock appear to portray a sacred marriage, the *hieros gamos*. Sometimes, as on Minoan seals from Crete, this is set in a boat, where a male and female figure are shown embracing, accompanied by axe-bearers. In one famous scene from Hitvlycke, a gigantic figure with an axe lifts it over a man and woman, and this is thought to indicate a ritual marriage, hallowed by the sacred symbol.

Plate 18

The towering axe-bearer who dominates the smaller figures has his male attribute clearly emphasized, and the conception of the sky-god as begetter and fecundator is confirmed by the emphasis on bull, stallion, ram and boar in the carvings, for all these at various times and in various regions have been chosen as manifestations of the male god of the sky. In Crete the marriage of god and goddess which caused the earth to bring forth was symbolized by an axe placed in a cave or cleft, and with this we may compare the axe buried below the floor of a house in the Late Neolithic period in Denmark.

Other weapons shown in the carvings are sword and spear. The sword appears frequently with the sun-disc, and is worn by the disc-men, but may have been the symbol of procreation rather than a weapon, for it seldom appears in scenes of conflict. It seems to be a religious symbol, carried on ships and sometimes shown alone with a worshipper. The spear however is often used in fighting scenes, and also depicted as if of enormous size, borne by a number of men. Spears are shown flying through the air, and a huge figure, apparently not identical with the axe-god, is depicted brandishing a spear. It is
Fig. 9
possible that this is a god of war, with a spear for his symbol, evolving separately from the god of the sky; but it seems more likely, from what we are discovering about early religion, that the different weapons represent varying aspects of the same deity.

Two symbols which may be associated with divine power are
Fig. 10
footprints carved on the rock, and the human hand or arm,

Fig. 9 Spear-bearer on rock at Litsleby, Tanum, Bohuslän (after Almgren)

sometimes of huge size. The feet may be bare or shod, and both they and the hand may be attached to ships, or placed over them. A raised arm might stand for worship, or authority; or again, it is possible that this is a symbol of the one-handed god, which Dumézil believed to be one of the earliest deities of the Indo-Europeans. A hand is seen on a Danish burial urn from Øster Hjerting, from the Late Bronze Age, and also on the keystone of a grave at Lille Havelse, so that there is some con- nection with the dead. Traces of feet might stand for the sign of a visiting deity, the returning dead, or the god touching earth in a thunderstorm, and both feet and hands are more likely to be symbols re-enacting the presence of a supernatural visitant than a record of human activities.

The chariot or wagon is often shown, either alone or with animals drawing it. The wheel came to the North in the Bronze Age, and must have seemed charged with significance and power. Besides the Trundholm disc on its wheeled carriage, we have an elaborate cauldron of bronze on wheels, from Skalle- rup, south Jutland, which held the cremated remains of a man, and was put in a tree coffin. The four spoked wheels resemble

Plate 20
Plate 21

sun-discs, and four birds are set on the shafts. It has been suggested that this was a sacred vessel used for rain-making, and
certainly the wheels and birds imply a link with the sky deity.
A chariot was sometimes used for divination in the ancient
world, as Tacitus records, and this practice may have been
known earlier in the North. Certainly the frequency with
which the wagon occurs and its appearance at Kivik suggest
that it played an important ceremonial role.

The plough too appears, both in the spade and crook varie-
ties, and is sometimes drawn by beasts. When shown with
horses pulling it, it is probably intended to be travelling in
procession, not in use in the fields. In the Bronze Age, it will
be recalled, ploughing formed part of funeral ceremonies.

The bull stands out from the various animals shown, and
many such, bearing impressive horns, are associated with
ploughs, ships, snakes and sun-discs. Occasionally the horns
meet to form a circle, suggesting a link with the sun-discs. Two
horned helmets were recovered from a bog at Vixø in Zealand
during the second World War; these are splendid objects,
with the smooth curved horns of the bull rising from them,
and the suggestion also of a bird of prey whose beak occurs on
the ridged crest. A small figure in a helmet of this kind, and
according to records bearing an axe in his hand when found,
has also survived from Denmark (see p. 60).

It seems that the bull was associated with special rites. In a
carving from Torsbo, Bohuslän, a man holds the horns and
seems to be vaulting over its back, and there are other parallels
to this, while in another scene a man is grappling with a bull
and forcing it to its knees. We know that the sky god was
represented by the bull over a large part of Europe, Asia and
Africa in ancient times, and that bull sports formed part of
religious ceremonies very early. They were apparently practised
in the Deccan and Southern India as early as the third millennium BC as well as in Bronze Age Crete.

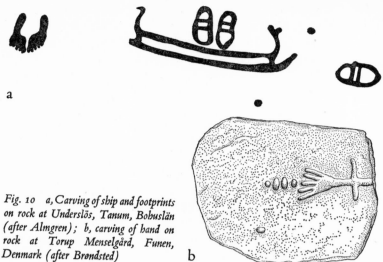

*Fig. 10 a, Carving of ship and footprints
on rock at Underslös, Tanum, Bohuslän
(after Almgren); b, carving of hand on
rock at Torup Menselgård, Funen,
Denmark (after Brøndsted)*

The boar also frequently appears, sometimes apparently
wild, at other times part of a herd; it is found associated with
the sword, and with ships. The horse is likewise associated with
wagon and ship. Whether it was used for riding as early as this
is questionable, and a few carvings thought to show men on
horseback may date from the close of the period. The stag
seems to hold a position similar to that of the horse, and some
horses are shown with horns, as if there was a tendency to
merge the two animals into one. Eleven gold bowls from Ma-
riesminde Bog, Lavingsgård, are believed to be imported objects to which alterations have been made by native craftsmen,
in the form of horses' heads with horns added to the handles.
In the Pazirik burials of the Altai in Siberia, whose date cor-
responds roughly with that of the late Bronze Age in Scandinavia, a set of artificial leather antlers was found on the head of a
horse's skeleton in one of the mounds. The sacred horned animal had long been venerated in the North, and the increasing

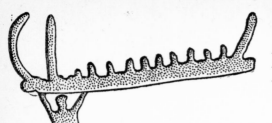

Fig. 11 Figure holding ship, on rock at Himmelstadlund, Norrköping, Sweden (after Almgren)

importance of the horse may have led to its investiture with the ancient symbol of power.

Most frequent of all symbols is the ship. This is sometimes held in the hands of a male figure, and may represent a votive offering. Evidently model ships were offered in this way, for a set of tiny ones, beautifully made of gilded bronze with con-centric circles on the prows, has been recovered from a clay jar in a bog at Nors, in Denmark. The carvings imply also that cult ships were carried or drawn in religious processions. In Egypt, where the ship of the sun was represented journeying across the sky and beneath the earth, ships formed part of of-ferings at the grave, and full-sized vessels were deposited near the pyramids of the rulers of the Old Kingdom. The idea of the journey under the earth might explain the importance of the ship in funeral ritual, and would link the sky-god with the dead committed to his care. Ship-funeral in the Bronze Age does not seem to have been a male prerogative, since women Plate 12 and children are found buried in tree-coffins. Increasing use of cremation may have strengthened the idea of the journey of the dead, but this is also linked with collective burial, since there is a widespread belief among people who practise it that the spirit is liberated from the flesh to pass to the realms of the dead (see p. 35). The wings of birds in cremation urns empha-size this idea of a journeying spirit, and echo the imagery of the many birds perched on sacred chariots of the Bronze Age from Central and Southern Europe.

Ships were not only means of travel, but a source of food, and from the time of the first settlement in Scandinavia, fishing was one of the chief ways of winning a harvest from the natural world. Some ships on the rocks have irregular shapes near them which may be fishing-nets, an emblem of fertility as important as the plough, and this may explain the fish on the Kivik slab.

Another ritual object appearing on the rocks is the musical instrument known as the *lur*. Dancing and leaping men are accompanied by others playing on these long, horn-like wind instruments which we know were in use during the Bronze Age. About fifty have been found in Denmark, showing how popular the instrument must have been, and a typology has been worked out from simple models to more elaborate ones with twisted tubes and a considerable register of notes. After the Bronze Age they disappear completely, and some of those in the bogs may be obsolete sacred objects abandoned when no longer in use. They had a powerful, resonant note when blown, and seem to have been used in pairs, by men standing or walking slowly, like the Scottish bagpipes. It is easy to visualize their use in religious processions and funeral ceremonies, or in summoning the people on solemn occasions.

Plate 17

FIGURES OF THE GODS

The symbols on the rocks cannot be studied in isolation. Sprockhoff has shown the importance of designs on bronze razors and other metal objects of the period, and how formal patterns have developed from the ship, horse and bird. All through the Bronze Age objects were left in holy places as before, and the bog-finds from the late Bronze Age include a considerable number of little metal figurines which appear to be anthropomorphic deities.

Although no ship models holding figures are known from Scandinavia, a wooden ship with several naked men standing erect was found at Roos Carr in Yorkshire in 1836. There were too many men for the boat, and it is thought that there were originally two vessels, each holding four men. The boat itself was shaped like a serpent with eyes of quartz, and the find was at first attributed to the Viking Age. In view of similar figures, however, some with quartz eyes, from Denmark, Sweden and Brandenburg, of known Bronze Age date, many scholars have accepted Lindqvist's arguments for placing the Roos Carr figures in this period.

Small metal figures of men and women may be survivors of elaborate ceremonial models like the famous cult wagon from Strettweg, near Judenburg, in Austria, which has a number of bronze figures grouped round a much larger female figure, believed to be the goddess of fertility. Some male figures from Scandinavia may have carried weapons, but in most cases their arms are missing, as from two small men found at Loshult in Scania, wearing loin-cloths and helmets with small holes which may have held horns. One figure, in a horned helmet like the Vixø ones, from Grevens Vænge near Næstved in Denmark, has survived, although he too has lost his right arm. New evidence is now available for the existence of a group in which he formed a part, for in two drawings made in 1778/9, he is shown as one of a pair kneeling side by side, each with an axe in the outside hand, while the arm on the inside is curved with the hand on the breast. A figure in the same posture forms the handle of a knife from Simris in Scania, but again the right arm is missing.

Of the four female figures found at the same time, only one now survives. She wears a short corded skirt and neckring, and bends back her head until it touches the ground, in the posture of an acrobat or dancer. The artists drew her as if she were flying through the air, but the backward posture appears to have been the intended one. The artists' notes indicate that there were two other similar figures, and also a fourth figure, standing, in a long skirt divided at the hem. This too appears to be a woman, as she has an earring on one side, and indications of breasts, and the drawing shows her on a stand on which there would be room for a matching figure to form a pair like the two helmeted men.

Other women in neckrings, and sometimes with earrings, come from Denmark. There is a kneeling figure from Fardål with right arm raised and left arm bent, the hand carefully modelled to show that the fingers are on either side of the nipple of her breast. She has large eyes of gold in her little bronze face, and her hair is cut short at the sides and falls in a short plait down her back. She was found with a strange snake-like creature with two gripping feet like birds' claws, which she may have been driving, as a cord is thought to have passed through her raised right hand and through holes in the animal's body and jaw. Three heads of bulls or horned horses were also found, and this set of figures, like the other, seems intended to form a group on a stand, perhaps on a boat or wagon.

Plate 25

An erect female figure with neckring and bare breasts, carrying a bowl, forms the handle of a knife from Itzehoe, Holstein, and there are others with neckrings from Javngyde, Fangel (kneeling, with hands on breasts), Farø, and Scania.

Plate 24

In this series of figures it seems that we are at last face to face with the goddess of fertility. The neckring and offering of the breast of the Fardål figure is fully in keeping with attributes of this goddess in the Mediterranean and Near East, as is also the conception of a driving goddess. The absence of this female deity on the rocks may be due to the fact that she presided mainly over women's mysteries and ceremonies connected with the dead. She may however have been symbolized by the serpent or the ship, both closely associated with her in other regions.

There is some evidence for her cult on cremation urns and from votive offerings. An urn from Maltegården shows a male and female figure, encircled by a neckring; it would appear that the goddess, identified by her necklace, is stretching

Fig. 12

Fig. 12 Lid of urn in sandstone, from Maltegården, Gentofte, Denmark, about 11 cm. across

Fig. 13

out welcoming hands to greet the dead. Of interest too is another Danish urn, where a figure with long hair, symbolizing the goddess, is merged in the familar shape of the house-urn. I would disagree with Brøndsted when he cites this as evidence for the meaninglessness of the symbols, for a strange combination of this kind is more likely to be deliberate, emphasizing the function of the goddess as receiver and shelterer of the dead, as in the megalithic tombs. Neckrings have been found in Denmark together with women's ornaments, as well as three separate finds of plaits of hair, which according to pollen analysis were deposited in the Bronze Age; one, from Sterbygård bog, Døstrup, consisted of seven plaits. Whether these were severed at marriage, at death, or to accompany some special petition to the goddess, we do not know, but they serve as a moving reminder of her power in a realm outside that depicted in the rock carvings.

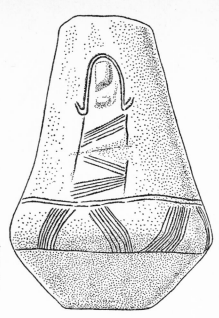

Fig. 13 Urn with figure of goddess combined with house motif, from Røgind, Viborgegnen, Denmark, about 35 cm. in height (after Brøndsted)

The new conception of religion, which probably found its way into Scandinavia in the late Neolithic period, spread gradually over the North in the course of the Bronze Age. The most important innovation is the emphasis on the god of the sky. The prominence of the sun-disc has frequently led to the statement that the main religion of the North in the Bronze Age was sun-worship, but this is based on theories about the development of religion now largely discredited.

The simple cult of sun-worship is no longer viewed as an inevitable first stage in man's religious development. Solar religions are rare, and are usually the products of advanced civilizations, where they develop as the special cult of a privileged class, as in Ancient Egypt, and exist along with many other types of worship. A special cult of the sun may possibly have existed among the leading warrior class buried in Bronze Age mounds in Denmark and Sweden, and in the use of symbols, and particularly that of the ship, there are striking parallels with Ancient Egypt. But there is no evidence to justify a theory of crude worship of the sun itself as a fertility power. Bronze Age religion was richer and more complex than this, and there are links with Minoan and early Greek cults, and an elaborate use of symbols on rocks, pottery and metal objects, in votive offerings and funeral customs, while figures appearing to represent the deities have been found in the Late Bronze Age in considerable numbers. These indicate that the chief divinity at this time is the sky-god, and this is confirmed by the importance of the axe, traditionally associated with thunder. Other gods connected with war or with the sea may have developed locally; or alternatively, the varying attributes of the supreme god of the sky may have led to a variety of emphasis. Since on the whole there is close agreement in the rock carvings over a wide area, it seems more likely that we are dealing with a god whose power extended over the agricultural world, the sea, the field of battle, and the land of the dead.

Although she plays no large part in the rock carvings, a goddess with bare breasts, a plait of hair, earrings and a neck-ring is vividly portrayed, and she seems to have taken over some of the character and attributes of the Great Mother of the megalithic peoples.

There are also symbols suggesting an invisible divine presence. Professor Bertil Almgren, of Uppsala University, has suggested that we should see the footprints on the rocks, the raised hand, the empty wagon and the unmanned ship as signs of the presence of a god, more effective perhaps than the groups of little anthropomorphic figures. Both god and goddess are honoured in funeral rites, but how far any conception of a journey made by privileged worshippers to join the gods in another world existed at this time, it is hard to say. No evidence survives to provide any clear picture of a world of the dead. The main interest of the men bearing aloft the sun-disc, leaping and dancing on the ships, and attending on the sacred animals appears to be the present world, where the life of farming, war and the sea was rendered significant and dramatic for them by the sense of the sacred which permeated it. Many must have cooperated in the ceremonies, processions, building of mounds and mock battles, and the rock pictures imply that an organized religion and professional priesthood lay behind these activities. They seem to be taking place in the open air, as we have no indication of temples or even enclosed places for the worship of the gods. The elaborate symbolism of the Kivik grave seems to stand alone, but the symbols used in it are linked at many points with the rock carvings, suggesting that an exceptional tomb of some great priest-king of this religion has chanced to survive in western Sweden.

We have as yet no knowledge of what change or breakdown in the way of life finally brought this rich religious activity to an end, so that the carvings ceased, and ritual objects were abandoned in the bogs. The remains of the next period, however, imply an abrupt break with what went before.

CHAPTER IV

The Great Sacrifices

THE FUNERAL FEAST

NOT FOR SOME TIME after the close of the Bronze Age did religious ideas of any vigour leave a mark on Scandinavia. In the fourth and fifth centuries BC there is a sudden dearth of archaeological finds. This has been explained in various ways: deterioration of the climate, the advance of the Celts which cut Scandinavia off from the south, or new fashions of burying the dead without grave goods. There may be some truth in all or any of these suggestions, though none of them seems adequate to explain the apparent lack of religious inspiration after so full and rich a period, the giving up of organized ceremonial, and the abandonment of sacred objects which were never replaced.

The main rite was still cremation, except for a few burials in Gotland in stone cists, sometimes in the shape of a ship. The ashes of the dead were usually placed in urns or buried in small pits, and the graves, sometimes on the site of the pyre, might be surrounded with stones, or marked by a low mound or cairn. Sometimes a lug was broken off an urn, possibly to dedicate it to the dead.

The careful separation of bones from ash after burning might be a continuation of the ancient tradition of freeing the spirit from the ties of earth. In the last two centuries before Christ however this was seldom observed, and the remains of the pyre were usually buried without separation. Traces of a 'death-house' are occasionally found, as if it were still customary to hold a second funeral ceremony. At Mandhøj on Bornholm a tent-like structure with wooden supports was raised over the cremated remains, and after a time this too was burnt and the remains covered by a mound.

Grave goods consisted mainly of ornaments worn by the dead, until two important innovations were introduced in the last two centuries BC. Weapons once again appear, and on the Swedish islands sickles are deposited in graves. It seems likely that both types of grave goods had symbolic value. From now until the end of the pagan period we find also intermittent examples of the custom of bending or breaking swords placed in the graves; Kragehede and other Danish cemeteries provide instances from the late Celtic Iron Age.

Kragehede also gives evidence for a new attitude towards the dead. They were now supplied not only with personal belongings, tools and weapons, but also with everything necessary for a banquet, and sometimes a wagon and horses were buried beside them. Other Danish cemeteries from widely different areas, such as Langå in south Jutland, reflect the same custom. Joints of lamb and pork and drinks of various kinds were placed in the grave, and at one burial at Skudstrup in the south, two drinking-horns provided were found to contain traces of mead and ale.

Mounting prosperity in Denmark was reflected in these graves, and with increasing richness of grave goods comes, for the first time since the Bronze Age, a sudden change from cremation to inhumation among the richest members of the community. At this time imports and influences were reaching Denmark from all directions, from the Roman Empire, from south-eastern Europe – particularly the region round the Black Sea – and from the Celtic peoples. It may well be Celtic influence that brought the custom of burial back into Denmark.

In north Jutland large stone burial chambers were built once more, an echo of ancient megalithic traditions, but with great stones rather than slabs. These were made to overhang by the principle of 'false vaulting' until they could be bridged by a stone at the top. Some of these tombs must have been family vaults, and grave goods are found at different levels, some perhaps originally left above the grave. Traces of wooden chambers have been found, and some kind of 'death-house' may sometimes have been built inside the tomb.

Above all, emphasis on the funeral feast continued in the first centuries AD. In the 'pottery graves' of east Jutland the dead lay in a single grave, accompanied by sufficient dishes, pots and cups to form a large dinner service. The body usually lay along the north wall with head to the west, arms outstretched as if to receive a share of the feast, with a cup within easy reach of the right hand; one woman was found grasping a wine-strainer. A large jug or pitcher and other cups stood near by, and more vessels at the foot of the grave, while in between stood dishes of meat and a knife. Other vessels are found higher up in the filling of the grave.

Such was the general plan for graves of men, women and children. It was not necessarily based on the crude notion that the dead continued to eat and drink under the earth, for such ritual could possess considerable symbolic meaning. Who were the other participants of this meal, prepared for several persons? Was it the living, who partook at the graveside, or the ancestors, welcoming the newcomer among them? The feast might well symbolize revelry in the Other World, when the traveller joined the hosts of the dead.

Funerals of this type can be traced back to the tombs of princely warriors of the Hallstatt culture, who were buried with a wagon, and with dishes and cups and joints of beef and pork in graves of the eighth century BC in Bohemia, Austria and Bavaria. These are thought to have been the leaders of a warrior society moving across Central Europe at the close of the Bronze Age. Classical authors and medieval Irish storytellers alike testify to the importance of ceremonial feasting among the Celts, and emphasize the significance of the chief-

Plate 27

tain's portion, the selected joint of meat which went to the most distinguished warrior. This suggests an alternative inter-pretation of the banquet in the grave, for if the dishes held the portion of meat suited to the rank of the dead, the array could be seen as a kind of insignia, like a medal on a soldier's breast or the sword as a badge of rank. The evidence certainly sug-gests that here we have the funeral rites of a princely warrior caste, taking pride in marks of social status, and assuming that the privileges of this world would continue beyond the grave. It may be assumed that eulogy and funeral dirge accompanied the feasting which ushered the chiefs of the Roman Iron Age out of this world, although of this there can be no survival.

Apart from the motif of the feast, there is considerable local variety in funeral ritual. Narrow inhumation graves are found in south Jutland, with walls of small stones, while cremation continued to be practised, and weapons were laid beside the ashes of the dead. The most impressive memorials of this period however were not from the graves, but from an elaborate series of votive offerings.

THE BOG-FINDS

Although the peat bogs provide finds from the Neolithic pe-riod onwards, the offerings deposited there in the Celtic Iron Age took on a different character and are on a much larger scale. The earliest is at Hjortspring, at what must have been a sacred place of the late Bronze Age, where wells were dug in the marsh. These proved to contain the bones of oxen, a large and a small dog, a sheep and a lamb. The main offering how-ever had been placed there about 200 BC, after climatic changes had caused a pool to form in the bog. Here lay a large war-canoe which could have held about two dozen warriors, with equipment for these and many more. There were approxi-mately 8 swords, 138 spears, 100 shields and 20 coats of mail, along with wooden utensils and tools, and the war equipment had been deliberately and extensively damaged. The boat had been dragged to the holy place and then apparently pelted with flints as it lay in the water.

This is something different from the slain animals whose bodies had been left in the marsh. The boat seems likely to be that of a vanquished enemy, loaded with booty taken in the fight, and it was sacrificed at about the time when weapons first appear in Danish graves. Offerings of war booty of this kind continued, and more than 20 small finds and six major ones which include weapons are known from Denmark. Four such finds were excavated in the last century, two large ones at Thorsbjerg and Vimose which date from the Roman period, and two more from Nydam and Kragehul from its close. In 1950 a fifthcentury find was excavated at Illerup, while at Ejsbøl Bog, Haderslev, thousands of objects of fourthcentury date have recently been discovered. These two last excavations, scientifically carried out, throw much light on conditions under which the largescale offerings were made. Small offeringplaces have been excavated also in Sweden, and work on one large one at Skedemose on Öland began in 1959.

The large offeringplaces are not entirely given up to battle sacrifices, and that at Thorsbjerg included gold rings, many small personal possessions, pottery, wooden objects and textiles. However, weapons make up a large part of the Danish finds, including swords, spears, coats of mail, shields, and bowsandarrows; these are found together with horse trappings, wagons, tools, farming implements, vessels, clothes and jewellery, and a number of boats. The Skedemose find, like that at Thorsbjerg, was slightly different in character, and included many arm and neckrings, pottery and wooden objects. It is noticeable that many articles are deliberately damaged: swords bent and broken, pottery smashed, shields and coats of mail cut in pieces, stones forced into metal vessels and also hurled at the objects as they lay on the ground. At Illerup weapons had been burned on a pyre and then smashed and bent before being carried to a pool in the bog, where some were thrown into the water and others left on the marshy ground. The finds at Skedemose also showed signs of burning.

The earlier finds seem to represent offerings made over a considerable period, many of which had lain in the open for a long while before they sank into the marsh. They were arranged in some kind of order, with clothes placed together and arrows tied in bundles, possibly because some of the booty had already been packed for transport by the enemy. At Haderslev two large collections of objects had been thrown into the water, and one of these, large enough to represent the equipment of an entire army, had sunk in confused heaps as if emptied out of sacks or buckets. Illerup seems to represent the equipment of about 70 warriors, destroyed at one time.

In the Roman period we have for the first time the evidence of literature to set beside that of archaeology, although this presents its own problems and cannot always be accepted at its face value. In the first century AD, Caesar described piles of booty left by the Gauls on consecrated ground, untouchable on pain of death. Four centuries later, Orosius, depending on some earlier source, describes the Cimbri as wrecking the treasure taken from the enemy, throwing gold and silver into the river and hacking coats of mail to pieces, while they drowned the horses and hanged the men whom they captured. Such abandonment and destruction of war booty is confirmed by the archaeological finds. Tacitus also tells us of German tribes of the first century AD, the Hermundari and the Chatti, vowing to offer up all that they won if their god would grant them victory. Such costly sacrifices must have demanded much of the warriors, but it seems that religious discipline and fear of the dread powers to which offerings were made were strong enough in Denmark to enforce this demand.

At the time of Tacitus the Germanic gods are believed to be Tîwaz and Wodan, called Mars and Mercury by the Romans. Tîwaz appears to have been the supreme sky-god, who also ruled the battlefield and established law among men. Wodan was the god of the dead, associated with magic and inspiration. The Celts in Gaul also worshipped a supreme sky-god with more than one function, who might be equated with Mars, Jupiter or Mercury. We do not know at what point during the Roman period a conception of a god primarily connected with the field of battle emerged, but it seems as if both Celts and Germans began by worshipping all-powerful deities, and later developed separate gods with more specialized functions. The sudden change to burial with weapons in the Celtic Iron Age and the deliberate sacrifice of war equipment may mean that a deity primarily associated with battle was emerging for the first time. It may be that Wodan, god of death, now became connected more particularly with war, and was worshipped by warrior leaders, so that the long-enduring tradition of feasting and unending combat in the halls of Odin, his northern counterpart, had its origin in this new development.

Both Celts and Germans appear to have believed in a group of fierce female spirits of slaughter who attended the god of battle. Such spirits are mentioned on altars together with Mars, and may be clearly differentiated from the female goddesses of plenty. Dedications to the German Alaisiagae, for instance, sometimes together with Mars, are found on two altars at Housesteads on Hadrian's Wall as well as on part of an arch or door-head, and there are Celtic dedications of a similar kind. These seem to have developed later into the Scandinavian valkyries and the minor goddesses of the Irish sagas.

It has already been indicated that by no means all the votive offerings were concerned with battle. Jankuhn claimed that Thorsbjerg was the holy place of the Angles, where offerings

were made for four or five hundred years, including those connected with agriculture and fertility. There are many unsolved
problems, like the reason for the death of the man from Tollund,   Plate 26
with his calm, impassive face and air of natural dignity, who
was found lying in a bog with a rope round his neck. A
woman from Borremose, whose body was similarly preserved,
had been clubbed to death. Whether these were sacrificial victims offered to Tîwaz or Wodan, criminals who had offended
the gods, or even rulers put to death to ensure good seasons,
we do not know. In view of the method by which the Tollund
man died, it is perhaps significant that those sacrificed to Wodan were traditionally hanged or strangled. Of the significance
of these sacrifices, archaeology can so far tell us little although
the large number of bodies recovered from the peat-bogs indicates that it may have been considerable.

THE TREASURES OF THE GODS

Some objects recovered from the bogs are in a class of their own
and seem to be ritual treasures, usually broken or dismantled
and placed in a small pit, as was the Brå cauldron, or on a
patch of dry ground fenced in from the bog, like the Dejbjerg
wagons. Such objects show Celtic influence, and are thought
by some to be of Celtic workmanship from Gaul or the Dan-
ube region. They confirm the importance of Celtic influence on
the religion of Denmark, and show also that a number of religious symbols first came into use at this time, when the Celts
and Germans were in close contact.

At Dejbjerg in west Jutland two highly decorated little wag-   Plate 28
ons were found in a bog in 1881 and 1883, and these are believed to have been made in the first century BC. The outside
frame was too fragile for much strain, but enclosed a stouter
wooden interior with a seat of wood and leather. The decoration was openwork sheet bronze fastened by nails, and included

abstract and geometric designs and small human faces with staring eyes and wavy hair set on the four uprights rising from the sides. Even poles and undercarriage were decorated, and the gleaming metal must have been effective against the wood.

Such wagons must have been intended for the transport of important people or for use in religious processions, and were possibly wagons of the gods, carrying on the Bronze Age tradition of transport of sacred objects in a wheeled carriage for worship and veneration. In this case the seat may have been intended for an image or for the priest or priestess in charge. The well-known passage from *Germania* 40, where Tacitus describes the worship of the goddess Nerthus by tribes believed to have lived in Denmark, gives a picture of such a sacred wagon in use. That of Nerthus was kept in a sacred grove, and none but the priest might look inside it. When the goddess was judged to have entered it, it was drawn through the land by oxen, while all fighting ceased amid general rejoicing, because this goddess, called by Tacitus *Terra Mater*, had returned to bring fruitfulness to men. After this the wagon and its contents were cleansed in a sacred lake, by rites so secret that the slaves performing them were afterwards put to death.

The Dejbjerg wagons could have had a cloth covering fastened to the uprights at the side, and been used in this way; but there is no evidence as to whether they were intended for god or goddess. Weaving objects found near by suggest women's rites, but may not have been deposited at the same time.

Another possible use for a wagon was to bear the dead to the grave, and burnt remains of wagons resembling the Dejbjerg ones come from a grave at Langå, where they were placed in a bronze cauldron, and from Kragehede, where a wagon was burnt with entire carcases of pigs and sheep, as well as the horses which must have drawn it to the grave.

Elaborate bowls and cauldrons, like that from Langå, also rank among the cult objects of this period. Several from the bogs are thought to be Celtic work, imported into Denmark, and the three most impressive of these are from Brå, in east Jutland, Rynkeby in Funen, and Gundestrup in north Jutland. It is difficult to date these; the Brå bowl is generally thought to belong to the third century and the Gundestrup bowl to the first century BC, although some would date them considerably later than this. On the Brå bowl are the heads of a horned animal and a bird of prey. Heads of bulls survive from lost bowls or cauldrons from Sophienborg and Rå, some gentle and others menacing, but all showing vitality and power. The peak of artistry, however, is reached with the work on the great silver vessel from Gundestrup.

Plate 35

On the base of this a bull-fight is depicted with the mixture of realism and stylization which marks the finest Celtic art. The powerful bull (whose horns are lost) occupies the centre, and stands out in bold relief. He seems to be sinking to the ground, though it has been argued that he is really intended to stand upright, stamping his feet and threatening the two surviving dogs after killing a third. But in any case the end is not far off, for above him hovers a swordsman, and it seems clear that this is the ritual killing which occupies the central sacrificial point of the bull cult.

Plate 29

Other plates inside the bowl show bulls threatened by men with swords and dogs, and it has been suggested that all these scenes are Mithraic in their inspiration; although these lively bull-fights with dogs are quite different from the way in which the bull's death is treated in Mithraic sculpture. Bull-slaying evidently occupied an important part in the religion of the Celts, and the number of bowls with bulls on them from Denmark implies that it continued there from the Bronze Age into the Celtic period. The horned helmet of the Bronze Age appears again, worn by a warrior with a wheel.

The stag is prominent on the bowl, and appears on one of the inside plates beside a man sitting cross-legged, who has been

Fig. 14

identified with the god Cernunnos on Celtic altars. He wears a torc round his neck, holds another in his right hand, and in his left grasps a horned serpent. The similarity between the man's horns and those of the stag implies a close link between them. The figure in its Buddha-like posture (a position familiar to the Celts and unlikely to be due to Eastern influence) has a remote, god-like dignity. The torc and serpent suggest association with prosperity and healing, and perhaps also with the dead. We may assume that the torcs worn by a number of figures on the bowl are more than mere ornaments, since they are frequently used for votive offerings and also deposited with the dead. They are worn by men as well as women in this period, and the rounded ends may be compared with those shown on the horns of bulls – apparently a sign of power. The transfer of the neckring to a male deity in this period may indicate the development of a male fertility god in the North, as companion to the ancient goddess.

Plate 30

The boar is shown on the Rynkeby bowl, as well as on the Gundestrup bowl, where it is grasped by two little figures; perhaps it serves as a battle-emblem or standard, for another warrior wears a helmet with a boar as crest. Stone figures of boars were set up by the Celts, and pork, one of the most esteemed dishes at the Celtic ceremonial feast, is often put into Danish graves.

Thus bull, stag and boar, animals of the herdsman and the hunter, are still important, and Celtic influence here may have reinforced earlier Scandinavian traditions. The horse appears only in a riding scene; a bird is to be seen in the hands of a female figure, and on the Brå cauldron. There are certain fabulous animals on the Gundestrup bowl, but these give a different impression, and Klindt-Jensen is probably right in suggesting that they are used to fill up space.

Certain figures on the bowl may be Celtic deities. One with a wheel is thought to be the god of the sky, equated with Jupi-

Fig. 14   Two figures from the inner plates of the bowl from Gundestrup, Denmark

ter on Roman altars, and possibly Taranis, god of sun and
thunder. The scene where a tall figure plunges a smaller one
head downwards into a cauldron might suggest a sacrifice, or a
descent into the cauldron of immortality, which formed one of
the treasures of the Celtic god known in Ireland as the 'Good
God', the *Dagda*. A female figure with long hair, bare breasts,
and a torc round her neck, surrounded by fantastic animals, is
likely to be the great goddess, whose worship must have continued into this period, and who is called Nerthus by Tacitus.

Fig. 14

There are altogether seven masks or busts on the outside of
the vessel, four male and three female, with one missing. Faces,
beards and hairstyles vary considerably, and some may be du-
plicates of figures inside the bowl. Although without very
clearly defined attributes, they possess authority and remoteness,
and a certain other-worldly air which seems to justify the claim
that they are supernatural figures. Evidence from other sources
confirms the picture of a multiplicity of gods and goddesses of

Plate 30

Fig. 15 Two wooden figures from Danish bogs, about 63 cm high. a, phallic figure from Broddenbjerg, north Jutland; b, female figure from Ræbild, Skovhuse, Himmerland (after Brøndsted)

a   b

the Celtic peoples, never simplified into a clearly defined pantheon like the Roman deities. One can say only that they seem to be associated with the sky, with battle, fertility and sacrifice, and that the horned god is depicted with special reverence. Other figures known to be prominent among the Celts, like the god with the mallet and the goddess of mares, are missing.

Very far removed from these dignified figures are two wooden ones from the close of the Celtic Iron Age, also recovered from the marshes. A phallic wooden figure, formed from a conveniently shaped piece of a tree, was found at Broddenbjerg near Viborg, with clay vessels, perhaps food offerings, beside him. He has a bearded head in the Celtic tradition. The other is a female figure from Ræbild, Himmerland, whose swelling body suggests fertility. They could be fixed upright in the ground, and could well stand for the old powers of fertility, worshipped by simple people in lonely places. There is a certain likeness to

Fig. 15

the wooden *seidi* of the Lapps, roughly carved wooden figures, often with only the face clearly defined, which were set up in the open and represented stream or mountain spirits.

None of the bowls, so rich in symbolism, bears a picture of a ship. The emphasis in this period seems to be on land rather than sea, an essential difference from the Bronze Age, if we are to judge from treasures like the Gundestrup bowl. We have some evidence for ship offerings in the bogs, although these may have formed part of those to the war-god. Not till later do we again find the ship as a major religious symbol.

THE WORSHIP OF THE WAR-GOD

The Celtic and Roman Iron Ages in the North form one of the most difficult periods in which to study the pagan religion in Scandinavia. There are many empty gaps, and evidence for religious practices is confused and incoherent, although a few points stand out clearly.

We gain the impression of a warrior cult which overshadows other aspects of religious life. This probably affected the rich men and warrior leaders rather than the mass of the people, as is ever the case with new concepts brought in by invading peoples. The wholesale sacrifices in the Danish bogs however show a startling unanimity on the part of the fighting section of the populace, although this does not seem to have been shared to anything like the same extent by the men of Sweden and Norway. As to the beliefs of women, children, old people and slaves, we have only hints from the account of the worship of Nerthus, and occasional offerings of objects other than war booty, for the continuing worship of the powers of fertility.

On the Celtic side we have a confused mass of evidence for the worship of many gods, from extensive archaeological remains and from classical, early Welsh and Irish literature. The ornaments on the great metal bowls must not be relied on too far, since they are probably imported material, but on the other hand they indicate the kind of symbolism which must have become familiar in Denmark, and the metal vessels which survive must be a small sample out of many ceremonial treas-ures of this kind. They may have symbolized the cauldron of plenty and immortality, or again they may have figured in ghastly sacrificial rites like those Strabo described among the Cimbri, when grey-haired priestesses in white linen cloaks and bronze girdles climbed a ladder to slit the throats of selected prisoners of war, catching their blood in a great bowl. Even if this was not regular procedure, we know that many animals were slain in this period as part of the funeral ritual and the bog offerings, while the existence of the man from Tollund (see p. 73) reminds us that hanging was a sacrificial rite among the Celts, associated according to Lucan with Taranis, and also among the followers of the Germanic Wodan.

Plate 26

The cult of a god of battles, with its emphasis on sacrifice for victory and on feasting in the halls of the god after death, may first have reached the North in this time of Celtic influence. The masculine fertility deity Cernunnos seems at least to have been known in Denmark at this period, and this may have been the origin of the male fertility deity in the North, although the rough phallic figure of wood found in the bog indicates a native cult among the humbler members of the population. Meanwhile the worship of sky-god and earth-goddess must have continued.

Confusing although this period is, it may well have been a very important one, since many symbols still familiar in the Viking Age seem to have come into prominence. We find the cauldron and the funeral banquet, sacrifice for victory, battle-spirits and goddesses of plenty, sacrificial hanging and divina-ation, as well as the already existing symbols of boar, wagon and sacred neckring. All these are associated in the mytholog-ical literature with the Æsir and the Vanir.

CHAPTER V

The Dancing Warriors

Leap for our cities, and leap for our sea-borne ships, and leap for our young citizens.
HYMN OF THE KOURETES

TREASURE IN THE EARTH

THE TIME OF THE MIGRATIONS of the Germanic peoples is one of the richest for Scandinavian archaeology, particularly in Sweden. From the fifth century onwards gold flowed freely into the North, coming through trade and also as part of the booty from the disintegrating Roman world. The exquisite gold treasures of delicate filigree work preserved in Stockholm show the splendid, ostentatious craftsmanship of this period, and the skill of the Swedish metalsmiths. Most of these treasures are not from graves but from hoards and deposits.

Hoards from all over Denmark provide numerous rings for fingers, arms and neck, gold bracteates, and treasures like the gold horns from Gallehus (see p. 84). Weapons and armour were still sacrificed, as at Haderslev and Illerup (see p. 70). Although there was a tendency to substitute a part for the whole, and to lay down a scabbard mount rather than a complete sword, the impulse for wholesale destruction, as at Illerup, was still strong. In Sweden hoards of gold are plentiful, ranging from the enormous treasure of broken metal and gold objects found at Tursholm in 1774 to small finds, and many of these appear to be votive offerings. This is especially true of objects like the golden horns and collars, although the possibility that these were the treasures of some sanctuary, hidden in time of unrest, must also be borne in mind. The finest gold collars, with human masks and tiny figures as part of their decoration, may have been intended for figures of the gods, or for their special devotees. A little bearded figure of wood from Rude Eskildstrup bog, sitting upright with a three-strand collar

Fig. 16

Plate 31

round his neck resembling those from the hoards, might be a miniature copy of an idol. The origin of such collars may be south-eastern Europe, for a huge neckring from the Black Sea area, too large for a human wearer, was included in a third-century hoard found at Havor in Gotland.

Alternatively, the collars may have been worn by men like the dedicated warriors mentioned by Tacitus among the Chatti, who wore iron collars round their necks in token of service to their battle-god. It may be no coincidence that a naked youth

Fig. 16

in a collar, with arms and legs in a dancing posture, appears on one of these splendid neck ornaments, from Alleborg. Gold rings might also form part of a battle sacrifice. Examples come from Thorsbjerg from about AD 300, and again at Skedemose, where seven gold rings weighing as much as 7 oz. each, and made about the fourth century AD, were found with swords, shield-bosses, spearheads and remains of horses and men.

A bog at Käringsjön, Halland, has yielded a different series of finds, recalling the life of farm, meadow and dairy, and continuing the tradition of Thorsbjerg (see p. 72). There were clay jars, some with traces of fat, which may have held part of the meat from sacrifices, farm implements such as ploughs and rakes, and remains of linen and spinning gear. As at Hjortspring, stones had been thrown at the sacrifices along with broken pottery (see p. 70). Charred branches in the water suggest that the offering took place at night, and that fires were lighted along the shore. Thus farming communities continued to make offerings in sacred lakes and lonely places.

Plate 34

At Braak in Schleswig-Holstein, two wooden figures found in 1947 suggest fertility cults of this kind. They are a naked man and woman, without neckrings, nearly one metre high, and roughly but effectively carved. The man may have been a phallic figure, but has been mutilated by a blow from an axe. There is also a series of small bronze figures of men, mostly

Plate 33

naked, from Denmark, at least four of which come from Funen.

Fig. 16 Dancing man, on golden collar from Alleborg, Sweden

Their bodies are crude, with sometimes only suggestions of limbs, but their faces, usually bearded, are made with some care, and resemble that of the figure from Rude Eskildstrup. One figure from Køng in Funen has runes on his body, apparently forming a word ending in *nga*. He may be compared with a small metal figure from Frøihov, Norway, probably belonging to the Migration period, which also bears two runic symbols and a third cryptic sign of runic type; he however is clad in a tunic or coat of mail and has a hat or helmet. This little man was found with a cremation in a bronze bowl, and was dated by Shetelig to the third century AD, although others have placed him later than this. Additional runes are said to have been scraped off by the finder, who hoped that the figure might be made of gold.

Plate 32

The little naked men might be votive offerings, associated with some sanctuary or cult centre on Funen, perhaps of a male fertility deity. They are not intended to be fastened on to a stand, like the Bronze Age metal figures, and are inferior to these in craftsmanship. Unfortunately they have no attributes which might identify them in any way, or link them with figures of Roman deities.

THE HORNS OF GALLEHUS

Outstanding among these hidden treasures were the golden horns from Gallehus, which merit comparison with the Gun-destrup bowl, since they were covered with figures and appear-ed to be associated with worship of the gods. The style of dec-oration and the runes on one horn date them to the early fifth century. The runic inscription in Western Germanic reads: *ek/hlewagastiR/holtijar/horna/tawido*, which is translated as: 'I, Legest from Holt (or 'son of Holt') made this horn.' This seems to establish them as objects made in the North and not imports from south-eastern Europe. The horns were found by local people near the village of Gallehus, north Schleswig, in 1679 and 1734, and must have lain near one another in spite of the long gap between the two discoveries. After some rough treatment they finally reached the king's collection of antiquities in Copenhagen, where they were kept as treasures and excited much interest in the learned world, while the intact horn was sometimes filled with Rhenish wine for distinguished visitors. Unfortunately, in 1802 they were stolen from a room above the Royal Library by a talented thief, Niels Heidenreich, who melted them down and made ornaments from the gold. We must therefore rely on drawings and descriptions made in the eighteenth century.

Fig. 18

Each horn consisted of an inner lining of plain gold, and a set of broad rings fitting over this, which the thief stated were of mixed gold and silver. These were covered with small figures and motifs, including incised figures of animals, birds, fishes, stars, rosettes and other ornamental motifs, which seem to have been purely decorative. There were also figures in relief which are believed to possess symbolic value, so that we have the same contrast between two types of decoration as on the Gundestrup bowl.

Ambitious attempts have been made to interpret the picture language of the horns. Worsaae saw them as figures from Eddic

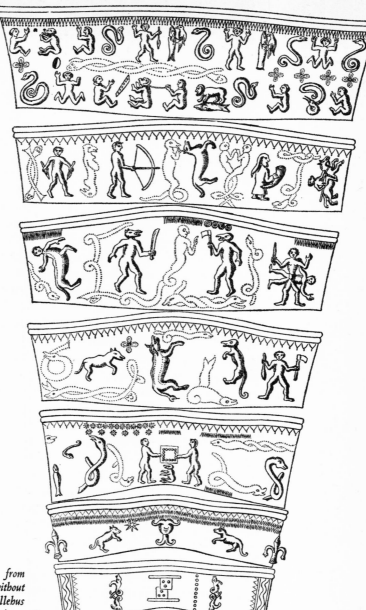

Fig. 17 Figures from the lost horn without runes, from Gallehus (after Oxenstierna)

85

mythology; Olrik thought they were also linked with Celtic tradition; Ringbom believed they represented dancers and acro-bats inspired by entertainments at the Hippodrome in Byzan-tium. More recently, Count Eric Oxenstierna has produced a detailed and scholarly study of the horns, collecting many paral-lels from the art of the classical and early Christian world, and evidence from seasonal rites and customs from medieval Scan-dinavia and Germany. While not accepting all his findings, I feel they must be treated with respect, and that it should now be possible to reach some general assumptions about the sig-nificance of the figure sequence.

The horns are clearly linked in subject-matter and manner of presentation, while some figures, like a man holding up another to form a cross, are found on both. Oxenstierna's main thesis is that, they show representations of the gods, and pic-tures of seasonal ceremonies connected with their worship, and thus would offer a parallel to the Gundestrup bowl. It may be that both bowl and horns were intended to hold the blood of sacrifice. Records show that the horns could be blown, but we also know that the intact one was used as a drinking-horn in the Danish court. Oxenstierna was surely right to emphasize the importance of the little long-haired figure on the second panel from the top of this horn, who may be either woman or priest, and who carries a drinking-horn. Adjacent to this is a four-footed animal, apparently a horse, which seems to be lying on the ground (it is at right-angles to the other figures) and beyond it an archer, aiming at the animal. Next comes a man with two weapons, pointing downwards, and another riding a horse. If we begin with the rider and finish with the figure carrying the horn, we have what could be a representa-tion of sacrifice, culminating with the offering of the victim's blood.

Oxenstierna suggests that this horn in concerned with the rites of autumn and winter, the other with those of spring and

Fig. 17

summer. This attempt to divide up the ritual seems to me the weakest part of his argument, since there are many indeterminate figures which have to be forced into the scheme. But certain scenes do suggest seasonal ceremonies. On the non-runic horn there are two men in animal-masks fighting, and beside them a centaur, which Oxenstierna sees as resembling the 'hobby-horse' of the mumming plays. The man holding up another could represent a sacrifice, or the recalling to life of the dead man, also found in such plays. The eyeless mask attacked by beasts could be the sun threatened by monsters. The figures in small groups divided by snakes in the top panel, who are engaged in dancing, ball-playing and acrobatics, could represent ceremonies to bring back the sun after winter darkness. Evidence from medieval and later records shows that such ceremonies existed in early times, and were either adopted by the Church or survived in popular seasonal customs.

Fig. 17

The runic horn has similar scenes. One panel has a hart and a serpent, both suckling their young, while an archer is aiming at them, which might represent a conflict between the powers of fertility and those hostile to them. A three-headed giant with a goat might be linked with the goat and its grotesque attendant which appear at weddings and yule ceremonies in various parts of Europe. Horsemen suggest the custom of riding the boundaries, which became part of the Rogation Day ceremonies. An archer who seems to be shooting at an animal skin with a human head above it is explained by Oxenstierna by the practice of shooting at a skin on a post, which was known among the Lapps, the Langobards, and elsewhere.

Fig. 18

Attempts to identify the figures on the horns with gods of the Migration period have been chiefly based on our knowledge of later Norse deities, but it seems sounder to approach them in the light of evidence from earlier periods. On the top panel of the runic horn are two figures, naked or wearing loin-cloths, who have helmets with curved horns resembling those of the

Fig. 18

Bronze Age. One holds a sickle and a rod, the other a short spear, a ring and a rod, and their legs are bent as if leaping or dancing. On either side of this pair is a warrior wearing a neckring and naked to the waist. They may wear loin-cloths, but it is difficult to be sure of this, since their bodies were set at the points where the chain attached to this horn was fastened. These warriors hold swords and shields, and also seem to be dancing. Between the pairs of men is an animal which is either a horse with crescent-shaped horns, or a hart.

Many scholars have claimed that this group represents the gods, and have attempted to identify the dancing men with Tîwaz, Wodan or Freyr. They have also seen Thor in the three-headed giant with a goat, Ull in the archer, and Tîwaz or Tyr in the one-handed figure found among the dancers on the non-runic horn. Such suggestions carry little conviction, chiefly because these figures give no impression of dignity or supernatural power. It seems safer to assume that these dancing, juggling, and riding men, wearing animal masks, fighting and shooting at a skin, are for the most part devotees of the gods, worshippers or priests, taking part in seasonal rites. I would see the men in horned helmets not as representations of idols from the temples, as Oxenstierna suggests, but rather as servants of the gods, wearing horns of power. Spear and sickle, ring and staff would link them with the deities of battle and fertility, like the figures on the Gundestrup bowl. The warriors with sword and shield would be the followers of the war-god.

It is interesting to note that here we have two sets of twins, recalling the pair of men in horned helmets from the Bronze Age, and twin dancers are found again, as we shall see, on helmets of the seventh century (see p. ooo). We have possibly a link here with the Twin Gods described by Tacitus, the sons of the sky-god, worshipped by Greeks and Romans, and shown on stones of the Roman period, usually accompanied by horses. Tacitus calls them the Alcis, worshipped by the Nahar-

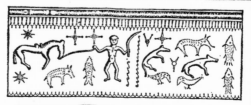

Fig. 18 Figures from the lost gold horn with runes, from Galle-hus, Denmark, from Paulli's drawing of 1734 (after Oxen-stierna)

vali in a forest sanctuary, and other writers state that they were worshipped by tribes near the North Sea. He describes them as young men and brothers, whose priests were decked out like women, but of whom no images were made, and we are told that they gave help to travellers. The men on the horn, carrying the sickle and spear, could express the double function of the sky-god and be his servants and supporters, known as his 'sons'.

The fertility goddess does not appear, but could be typified by the female animals with young. Figures of a doe and her young are found in Norwegian women's graves of this period, and resemble the animals on the horn. The ring and the snake could be in keeping with the male fertility deity on the Gunde-strup bowl.

The emphasis on the horse sacrifice seems to be new. This ceremony can be studied in detail in the Brahmin rites of India, and here it was essentially the cult of a ruling warrior caste. In spite of strong sexual emphasis in the Vedic rites, they were not primarily associated with the earth-goddess, but formed part of the worship of the sky-god, and the horse represented the universe. It replaced the bull of an earlier cult, and the same process seems to have taken place in Denmark. The importance of the horse sacrifice in Scandinavia at this time is confirmed by finds from Skedemose, where offerings continued to be made until the end of the fifth century. This find, unlike the Danish ones, contained many horse bones, both complete skeletons and heaps of ribs chopped in pieces. It seems that horse sacrifice took place here, and perhaps horse-racing too, if one interpretation of the name *Skedemose* is correct. We may note in this connection the man standing by a horse and the horse-rider on the Gallehus horns.

Fig. 19

On the Häggeby stone from Uppland, Sweden, a horse-fight is clearly pictured, and the animals, urged on by two men, have horns on their heads. More traces of ritual have been found by Klindt-Jensen on the Island of Bornholm, in excavations of

Fig. 19   Carved stone from Häggeby, Uppland, Sweden, now in the Historiska Museum, Stockholm. Probably fifth or early sixth century

a house of the Migration period at Sorte Muld. A pit outside the house held the head of a horse, four severed feet and bone from the pelvis; these bones, unlike ordinary household refuse, had not been gnawed by dogs. Sets of horses' skulls and hoofs have also been found in a peat bog at Rislev in Zealand, and in a cone-shaped pit beside a grave at Leuna in Germany, and Klindt-Jensen gives other possible parallels from Central and South-East Europe. It is possible that the ritual of horse sacrifice came into Scandinavia during the Migration period by way of the Baltic islands.

Thus, although it is not yet possible to explain convincingly all the figures on the horns, we can go some way by comparing them with symbols and rites of earlier periods, and the parallels with the Gundestrup bowl are especially valuable. Other parallels will emerge from the helmets of the Vendel period (see p. 96).

a

GOLDEN AMULETS

Figures which provide further problems in identification are those on the gold bracteates, hanging ornaments originating in Scandinavia as copies of Roman medallions, but soon developing on lines of their own. They were so popular that they survive in hundreds from Denmark, Sweden and Norway, and in smaller quantities from neighbouring countries. They were evidently used as amulets, since they bear such runic inscriptions as 'Luck for Alvin', or 'I give luck', and the copying of the Emperor's head on the Roman medallions may have come about in order to extend the luck and protective power of this semi-divine ruler to those who wore his image. It is the variations on this image, however, that are significant.

The bracteates are divided into four main groups for convenience of study; more elaborate classifications given by

Fig. 20 Gold bracteates: (a) Alingås, Västergötland, Sweden (260); (b) unknown site, Denmark (338); (c) Bolbro, Odense, Denmark (56); (d) Kongsvad Aa, Pr`æ`stø, Denmark (36)

Mackeprang (to whose work the numbers in brackets refer) need not concern us here. The earliest group, A, probably belongs to the fifth century, when many gold coins were reaching Denmark, and is based on the emperor's head. Bracteates of group B show several figures, originating from Roman models of Victory crowning the hero, and those of group C a man on horseback, again based on figures of the emperor. The treatment of these two groups is however far from classical in style. These are probably late fifth- and sixth-century in date, while the last group, D, consists of bracteates with abstract animal ornament of Style II, probably belonging to the late sixth, and early seventh century.

Fig. 20b
Fig. 20a

Attempts have once more been made to identify figures in groups B and C with gods like Odin, Thor, Freyr and Tyr, and also with the hero Sigurd the Volsung. To me, however, it seems mistaken policy to attempt to force these vigorous, confused little pictures into preconceived mythological schemes. The intention does not seem to be the portraying of myths or legends, but rather the inscribing of symbols of power, which would naturally be associated to some extent with the gods.

The horse is clearly important, and has features not taken from Roman models, in particular crescent-shaped horns on its fore-

93

Fig. 20a

head, like the animal on the Gallehus horn. This is shown on a bracteate from Alingås, Västergotland, which also has a swastika above the horse's head. Sometimes a bird is shown with the rider, and also appears on B bracteates along with the figure of a dancing, leaping or running man. He is shown

Plate 36

clearly on a Danish bracteate now in the University Museum at Oslo, accompanied by horse, bird and swastika. On this bracteate the animal appears as a horse, but on others it resem, bles a wolf or dragon, and on one bracteate from Hamburg, Egnen (322) a man is shown with upraised sword and his hand between the creature's jaws. Sometimes the bird is re,

Plate 36

cognizably an eagle, and there is a series of bracteates, to which the Oslo example belongs, where the hair of the emperor is changed to a curved head,covering which suggests a helmet, and which ends in a point shaped like an eagle's head. An,

Fig. 20c
Fig. 20b

other example is from Bolbro, Odense.

Less common figures worth noting are a man holding a double axe, as on bracteate 338 from Denmark, an archer, as on 110, and a set of three bracteates from Å, Præsto (36) which

Fig. 20d

show a head with a child's head beside it.

The man on horseback is simplified to a head only, but the dancing youth appears in entirety, wearing only headdress and belt. He has no consistent attributes to identify him, for while the eagle suggests Odin, the horse could belong to Odin or Freyr, and the swastika to Thor, if we depended on symbols of the Viking Age. It is probable, however, that these amulets in, clude symbols of different cults, and were not in general intend, ed for worshippers of one deity only. They show at least that the swastika and the eagle were by now well established in Scandinavia, and both symbols primarily suggest association with the god of the sky. There is little indication of interest in the fertility goddess, and women are left out of the picture. We may further note the similarity between the dancers in horned helmets and the dancing youth of the bracteates.

Yet women have their place on another series of gold amulets, small rectangles of gold foil known as *guld gubber* (gold
grandads) from Denmark, Sweden and Norway, which seem
to have been used from the Migration period to the Viking
Age, although exact dating is difficult as they have been found
chiefly on house sites. The most characteristic motif is of a man
and woman facing one another, sometimes embracing. They
wear elaborate clothes and their knees may be bent, leading
Holmqvist to conclude that they are taking part in a formal
dance. He has, moreover, found pendants showing pairs of
women dancing, and in one case two men, to strengthen his
argument.

These little scenes, however, strongly suggest some kind of
cult not represented on the bracteates, and Grieg's comparison
with the *Dalarpenning*, the amulet worn by the Norwegian bride
at her wedding and bridal night in medieval times in Norway,
seems highly relevant here. These bore figures such as Christ,
Mary, and St Olaf, and were worn to bring blessing and good
luck to the union. The tiny gold plates could have been sewn
into wedding clothes, and the elaborate array of the couple
could represent bridal finery, while the dancing figures would
also be consistent with such a use, since the dance was an important part of wedding festivities. The branch or twig sometimes appearing between the couple emphasizes this ritual
aspect, and this could indeed be a naive representation of the
divine marriage, such as seems to be indicated in the Bronze
Age carvings (see p. 54). The amulets which consist of single
figures, far fewer in number, could, as Nordén suggests, have
been used as love tokens.

Mackeprang saw a possible link between these plates and a
tiny gold figure from Trønninge, Holbæk, in Denmark, resembling a small, squat idol, with a cloak which appears to be of
feathers. He is skilfully modelled, and might represent another
aspect of the male fertility god who appeared in the Roman

Plate 38

Plate 39

period, while it may be remembered that in the literature the 'feather-form' was one of the possessions of the Vanir, used by Freyja.

THE EAGLE AND THE BOAR

The Vendel period, extending from the late sixth to the late seventh century, takes its name from the cemetery of Vendel in Sweden (see p. 114). From here and from other sites comes a rich array of weapons, no longer found in bog deposits. In particular there are a number of splendid helmets, decorated with metal plates, and four dies used in making such plates have been found at Torslunda on the island of Öland. The implication is that the plates bore standardized motifs, and so offer valuable evidence for the popular symbols of the period.

On helmets from graves I and XIV at Vendel are depicted warriors in helmets which have either an eagle or a boar for a crest, while two warriors with boar crests appear on a Torslunda plate. The eagle may have been imitated from ceremonial helmets in the Roman army, like the one dredged up in the River Wensum in England, but certainly by the sixth century AD it had become a dominant sign among the Germanic peoples. It appears on several fine shields, like those from Vendel I, the Lombardic shield from Ischl, and the shield from Sutton Hoo, while large numbers of eagle brooches survive from Germanic territory. We know that the eagle was associated with Wodan, god of the dead, to whom sacrifices were made on the battlefield, and it seems a very fitting symbol. He was the god who travelled far over land and sea; he inherited some of the prestige of the emperor with whom the eagle was associated, in his position as leader of the gods and divine ancestor of kings; while the eagle and the raven were beasts of prey who feasted on the slain.

Plate 41

Plate 40
Fig. 21

Plate 41

Fig. 21   Figures from helmet plates from graves 1 and 14 in the cemetery at Vendel, Sweden, showing helmet crests in the form of boars (after Arne)

The boar on the other hand was associated consistently with the Vanir, the deities of fertility. From the Roman period he was widely used as a protective sign on armour and weapons, and was used by the Anglo-Saxons on both helmets and swords. According to the literature, he was a favourite emblem of the early Swedish kings, for several of these are said to have possessed boar helmets which were national treasures. Both Freyr and Freyja, the chief Vanir deities, were said to possess golden boars, and when in one of the Edda poems Freyja's worshipper is said to take the form of her boar, this may allude to the wearing of a boar helmet like that from Vendel XIV, which has protruding tusks and resembles a boar mask. Boar helmets may have come into Scandinavia with the Celts, since one is shown on the Gundestrup bowl. There is no doubt that both eagle and boar were believed to be protective symbols for warriors in battle, and that while the Vanir stood for peace and plenty, the male god of fertility was also associated with war and the battlefield.

Plate 42

We find also on the helmet plates the now familiar motif of a dancing youth. He appears on one of the Torslunda dies with a spear in each hand, wearing only a belt, a sword on the shoulder, and a helmet fitted with horns which curve round to meet at the top, and which end in beaked heads. The same type of headdress appears again on a plate from the Sutton Hoo helmet (believed to have been made in Sweden), where it is worn by two warriors in short coats, holding crossed spears in one hand and a sword in the other, who also seem to be dancing, while traces of a similar pair have been made out on fragments of plates from Valsgärde 7 and from one of the mounds at Old Uppsala. In 1965 Sonia Hawkes published a buckle from a

Plate 37

seventh-century grave in the Anglo-Saxon cemetery at Fing-lesham in Kent, showing a naked youth in a helmet of the same kind, believed to have been made in Kent under Swedish influence. A similar figure appears on yet another helmet plate from grave VIII at Valsgärde, this time in a battle scene show-ing a rider whose steed is being stabbed by a warrior lying on

Fig. 22

the ground. This scene also appears on the Sutton Hoo helmet and on a brooch from Plieshausen, but it is clearest on the Valsgärde plate, where the naked youth is apparently leaping behind the rider and grasping his spear, suggesting that he is an emissary of the god of death, Wodan or Odin, guiding the spear of the warrior about to fall in battle, and thus deciding his fate. The fact that here we have a male figure on the battle-field, not the female Valkyrie of Old Norse literature, is a point to which we must return later (see p. 130).

The leaping or dancing youth is clearly a familiar figure in this period. He wears only a helmet and belt, and we know that the practice of fighting without defensive armour was charac-teristic of certain German warriors in the time of Tacitus, while in Viking times it was the custom of the berserks who followed Odin. Tacitus also stressed the importance among the Germans of a dance performed by naked youths, between

Fig. 22   Helmet plate from grave 8 at Valsgärde, Sweden (after Arwidsson)

'upturned swords and spears', and it seems that it is to such a milieu as this that the figures in the curved helmets belong. The upright horns on helmets of the Bronze Age are now replaced by curved horns ending in beaked heads, probably on account of the popularity of the eagle symbol at this period.

The helmet plates also show figures with animal heads and fantastic beasts, which may perhaps be linked with some of those on the Gallehus horns. A wolf-headed man appears on a Torslunda die, beside an animal figure on a chain, who reappears in a different guise on a plate from Vendel I. Another Torslunda die shows a man in a coat of mail between two animals whose jaws seem to be closing on his head, as he plunges a sword into the body of one of them. There has been much speculation as to the meaning of these scenes, and whether the creatures are bears, wolves or dragons, but there is little to connect them with any known myth or story. It seems more probable that like the Gallehus men they are in fact performing ritual actions, and that this gives them a symbolic meaning so that their presence on the helmet brings luck and protection to the warrior who wears it. There is probably some

Plate 41

99

link with the berserks of later literature, those picked champions who fought naked or in skins of wolves or bears, and who were under the special protection of Odin in battle. Ritual dances may well have been performed by such warriors, or by men mimicking them, for there is a reference in the *Book of Ceremonies* of the Emperor Constantine VII to a 'Gothic dance' of this kind performed by members of the Varangian guard at Byzantium, when warriors taking part wore animal skins and masks.

The chained monster may be associated either with Odin, who was the god with power to loose and to bind, or perhaps in an earlier period still with Tîwaz, the god who chained the wolf, remembered in the Viking Age as Tyr. The chains laid by Odin on his enemies were fetters of the mind, rendering men helpless at a crucial moment in battle, and a plate which may represent symbolism of this kind is that of a fettered man on the scabbard of a sword from grave VII in the cemetery at Valsgärde.

The helmet plates surviving from this period show a wealth of symbolism associated with battle, and indicate that the cult of Wodan/Odin continued to flourish in Sweden, together with that of a god with the boar as his emblem. The link with the symbolism of the bracteates emphasizes the importance of this warrior world, where luck mattered so intensely, and where the depicting of ritual actions was itself of importance for the promoting of victory.

THE PAINTED STONES

On the Baltic island of Gotland there is a unique series of carved stones, some of great size, bearing symbols and pictures, which were set up over a period extending from the Migration period to the eleventh century. The figures are chiselled out from the background, and traces of colour show that they were originally painted. Lindqvist points out that the effect of the more elaborate stones must have been like that of a great oil-painting, and that details of clothes and faces painted in would have made the scenes far easier to recognize. Now however only the silhouettes are left, often roughly treated by the weather. Some stones still stand in the open; others were built into church walls, while some have been found under the floors, like the magnificent stone from Sanda discovered in 1954.

Plate 46

Lindqvist dates the earliest stones from about AD 500, which would place them in the same world of heathen thought to which the Gallehus horns and the helmet plates belong. The inspiration behind them is probably the memorial stones and sarcophagi of the Roman Empire, and Lindqvist has found two close parallels from Spain, though it is probable that the main motif shown on the Gotland and Spanish stones came from South-East Europe. This is a great circular design which occupies the upper part of the stone; it seems to represent a whirling disc, with occasional variations in the form of spiral patterns or a swastika built up of curved lines, as on a stone from Hablingbo Havor. There may be two smaller circles, filled with spirals or a rosette pattern, beneath the large one. Many stones are incomplete, but the full-length ones usually have the outline of a ship below the circles, a long low vessel manned by rowers, executed with a vigorous economy of line suggesting long practice.

Plate 46

Small figures of men and animals are also found, utterly different in style from anything on Roman memorial stones. Some are warriors, and those on a stone from Vallstena carry spears and raise decorated shields which resemble the discs on the stones; others are men on horseback. There are also strange animals: horses with horns and fantastic biting jaws, as on a stone from Väskinde found in 1953, and monsters which suggest dragons, with thicker bodies and more elaborate heads than serpents. The small discs sometimes end in serpentine or

Fig. 23

Plate 46

dragon heads, and the stone from Havor has a stylized row of monsters with long protruding tongues forming a border. A particularly vivid monster is pursuing a small naked man on a stone from Hangvar Austers. The Sanda stone has one feature so far without parallel, a tree which appears below the discs and with a monster and a ship.

The stones are presumably memorials to the dead. Some were erected in small groups, and others within a low circular cairn of stones, with some low ornamented stones for a border, as in reconstructed examples from Hellvi Lilla Ihre and Väskinde. There was a cremation grave at Väskinde, and at Buttle a cremation cist in front of the stone. Some stones might be memorials to men lost at sea, or abroad, and some of the later stones with runic inscriptions certainly commemorate men who died away from Gotland; it has been suggested that they were erected as a legal proof of death. This might explain the introduction of the ship, although another explanation of this is that it originated from the boat-shaped moon seen with the circular disc on some Roman memorial stones.

To find parallels to the designs on Roman stones does not however explain their significance to the Gotlanders. Such symbols would not be chosen merely to form attractive designs, but because in the beginning they were thought to be powerful symbols, even if they became outworn conventions later. On Roman stones the disc appears to represent the sun, sometimes with the moon and planets below it. A comparison here may be made with the wheel of the Celtic sky-god, and it seems likely that the disc was linked with the sky deity. If this design were an important one, it may well have occurred also on shields of this period, like those pictured on the Vallstena stone.

The devouring monsters are likely to be associated with the kingdom of death, continuing the serpent tradition of earlier periods. About this time, dragons appear on Swedish shields from Vendel, the finest example of all surviving on the great

Fig. 23   Monster on stone from Hang-var Austers, Gotland (after Lindqvist)

ceremonial shield of Sutton Hoo. The ship motif is new, al-though it was closely connected with the sun in Bronze Age times. It must have been of great importance, since it continues up to the Christian period, and it is hardly possible to argue that all these stones were put up for travellers lost at sea. The Häggeby stone from Uppland, which shows the horned horses, has a ship on its reverse side, presumably in the same tradition.

Fig. 19

The tree is of great interest, suggesting the image of the World Tree, a central motif in the mythological sources. A tree appears on a cremation urn from Nitzahn in Branden-burg, along with a swastika and equal-armed crosses, and it seems that the swastika, here and elsewhere, replaces the whir-ling disc or wheel. There is a series of elaborate swastikas on Anglo-Saxon cremation urns from East Anglia, and a parallel example from Norway is on an urn from Vestfold, in the museum at Oslo.

Plate 46

Plate 45

Besides the series of large stones, there are several smaller ones, thought to date from the fifth century, much cruder in workmanship. The ship appears, but is a less elegant vessel, and with it a new motif in the form of one or two birds shaped like geese or ducks, again offering a striking resemblance to *Fig. 24* Bronze Age symbols. The emphasis here may be on the journey of wild geese or ducks across the sky, so that like the ship they serve as a fitting symbol of the journey of the dead. There is also a four-footed animal with horns, either stag or horned horse, and two horses face to face appear on a slab from Eskel-hem Larsarve, recalling the horses on the Kivik grave slab (see p. 50).

Parallels to the smaller stones are found in Uppland, but most of these have simple abstract patterns. Another form of memorial found in Uppland and Gotland is the carved stone sphere, sometimes found beside a standing stone. A particularly elaborate example comes from Inglinge Howe near Växsjö, and its elegant spiral ornament has led Nerman to argue that both it and the howe itself belong to the Bronze Age. This stone traditionally stood in front of a tall upright stone, and was known as the 'King of Värend's throne'. Lindqvist has collected evidence for such stones alternating with upright memorial stones on several great burial mounds of the Vendel period, and they must have possessed some ritual significance. One *Plate 43* from Pilungs in Gotland has a simple version of the whirling motif, showing its resemblance to a swastika. The design on the spheres is usually simple, although one in the Upplands Museum at Uppsala, partially reconstructed, has horses on it.

The spherical stones have a flattened base and top, and sometimes the top is sliced off to give the stone the shape of a cheese. It seems likely that such a shape was intended for a seat for someone taking part in rites connected with the howe, or in Gotland with the family grave. Olaus Magnus refers to a special stone called *Moraston*, at Uppsala, on which the new king

Fig. 24 Bird on stone no. 7 from Halla Broa, Gotland (after Lind-qvist)

was placed; this he describes as 'rounded' (*rotundus*). The spherical shape may have been adopted so that the stone would roll easily down the mound, as the Inglinge stone has often been rolled down in modern times. There may here be some link with the popular custom of rolling wheels and eggs down hills and mounds as part of Easter or spring rites in many parts of Western Europe, while again there is a well-known story in *Heimskringla* of a Norwegian ruler who gave up his kingship, and 'rolled' himself down from his ancestral mound to a lower position as a jarl. In Gotland, where mounds were not erected, the sphere has no obvious function; it was soon replaced by standing stones.

The memorial stones in Gotland show how in one small is-land certain symbols became firmly associated with the dead, particularly some of those used in the Bronze Age but apparent-ly forgotten over a long period. Gotland forms a bridge between

Sweden and the East, and it is possible that some of the symbols re-entered the North by this road. Further development in symbolism took place in the Viking Age, as we shall see (see p. 124).

THE HOUSE OF THE DEAD

While there is not much evidence for elaborate funeral ritual in the early Migration period, it was evidently important for leaders among the people to be given an impressive burial mound after death. Since many of these burials have been plundered, dating is difficult, but a number of imposing graves from Norway and Sweden, consisting of wooden burial chambers within large mounds, are thought to belong to this period. The earliest is probably the mound at Lillar Jored, Bohuslän, while the Sætrang grave in Ringerrike, excavated in 1834, is thought to date from about AD 375. This was a double grave, holding a man and woman in rich clothes, lying on bear skins and supplied with jewellery, weapons, gaming pieces, drinking vessels, wooden buckets and pottery. The excavator claimed that there were two separate chambers, one in the shape of a rhombus holding the bodies, a second, triangular in shape, in which vessels of clay, glass and wood were placed; later archaeologists have however expressed doubt as to whether his observations are wholly reliable.

Plate 47

The shape of the cairn is shown in two surviving plans, and it seems unlikely that the artist imagined so unexpected a structure as a cairn of stones shaped like a four-pointed star with curved ends. Dr Slomann points out that no parallel to this is known. Yet it is the same shape as that on one of the Gotland spheres, and bears a striking resemblance to the device of the whirling wheel and the swastika. It may be recognized again

Plate 44

in the shape of a metal ornament from Gjone, Vestfold, with whirling arms suggesting flames.

There has been much debate as to whether the wooden burial chambers of this period originated in South-East Europe, Germany, or some part of the Roman Empire. There may have been a tendency to emulate foreign burial customs, but on the other hand the wooden house of the dead was a familiar feature from Neolithic times onwards, and was even used in a somewhat different form for cremation funerals, as is shown by the evidence from Old Uppsala.

The burial mounds at Old Uppsala are the most famous of the period. Three huge mounds and one flat-topped artificial one, not used for burial, stand near the medieval church. The central mound is believed to have been built in the fifth century and enlarged about a hundred years later. The eastern mound is probably early sixth-century, roughly contemporary with another mound, Ottar's Howe at Vendel, north of Uppsala. The western mound was built last, about the middle of the sixth-century. Nerman's theory that these mounds hold the remains of three early kings of Sweden, remembered in *Beowulf* and *Ynglinga Saga*, is now generally accepted. According to this, the central mound is the grave of King Aun, the eastern mound that of his son, Egil or Ongentheow, while Egil's son Ottar is buried in the mound which bears his name at Vendel, and Ottar's son Adils in the western mound. According to literary sources, Ottar was said to be buried at Vendel in Denmark, but this is now thought to be an error caused by similarity of name.

Few grave goods survived the cremation, but even without the literary evidence it is clear that these were important graves. Lindqvist's excavations at Old Uppsala show that the dead king, possibly with a companion or slave, was burned in some kind of wooden house. That of the eastern mound seems to have been a wooden erection shaped like a wigwam, resembling beacons used in Sweden in later times, or charcoal burners' huts in Germany. The central mound had a heavier

Plate 48

Fig. 29

timber structure raised on stones. In each case the funeral pyre was erected on a large flat bed of clay, with stones beneath to produce a draught under the fire. Grave goods seem to have consisted of personal ornaments, small gold and bronze objects, combs, glass vessels, whetstones and in each case a set of gaming-men, while at least one helmet plate was recognized; but such great heat was produced that little survived.

Animals were killed with the dead, although not in large numbers. Traces of dogs have been found, but other remains may merely be from joints of meat used at the funeral. It cannot be established whether the second person burned was a man or a woman.

After the burning the bones were collected and washed, then buried in a simple clay urn or wooden bucket in a cavity in the ground at the place of the pyre. Stones were then heaped over it to form a large cairn, and above this the howe was built of earth covered with turf. The mounds were given flat tops, and the western mound and Ottar's mound at Vendel had sloping tops resembling a stage, action on which would be easily visible to people gathered in front. There seems little doubt that ceremonies were held at these royal graves. The Thing, or local assembly, met at Old Uppsala until the six-teenth-century, and the borough moot was held for many years on the flat-topped mound beside the tumuli called Domar-hogen or Tingshogen. The temple of the gods later stood near the mounds, but it appears that in the fifth and sixth centuries the sacred centre was the tomb of the dead king. The sanctity of the burial mound of king and landowner continued into the Viking Age, and many traditions have survived in the litera-ture of kings and seers sitting on the mound to claim succes-sion, to obtain wisdom from the dead, or to proclaim laws to Plate 49 the people. The impressive Tynwald Hill at St John's on the Isle of Man, with its various levels for men of different ranks and a seat for the monarch at the top, is a survival of the mound as the seat of authority in pagan times. Although Tynwald is not itself a burial mound, it has been placed on the site of an earlier mound of the Bronze Age, and has pre-Christian graves in its vicinity. If Inglinge Howe, as is generally believed, is a mound of the Migration period (see p. 104), then this also was set upon the site of an earlier tumulus of the Bronze Age. Here too the local Thing was held, and the main howe is surrounded by smaller graves and by stone-settings of various kinds, some probably much older than the howe itself.

Lindqvist has suggested that the elaborate wooden building forming the funeral pyre was in imitation of the cremation ceremonies of the Roman emperors, and that the line of mounds at Uppsala might be modelled on tombs along the Appian way. But as with the memorial stones and gold bracteates, ideas from Rome were no doubt adopted precisely because they fitted in so well with the existing traditions of Northern religion, and they were adapted accordingly. The most vigorous symbolism of the period between the fifth and seventh centuries, in which various new practices seem to have entered the North, is that associated with Wodan, the Germanic god of magic and the dead, whose cult was now adapted for aristocratic warriors. The eagle symbol appears to be his, and possibly also the Gotland symbol of the turning wheel or flashing disc. We know that Wodan was the god who sent men madness, and that he was held to give inspiration and intoxication to his followers, in particular that form of possession which led them to fight with utter fearlessness and abnormal strength. To this cult also it would seem that the dancing warriors belong. It appears that at the time of his greatest prestige Wodan took over some of the attributes and symbols of the sky-god, and these were wrested from Tîwaz; certainly, fire was traditionally associated with his cult in Sweden, and according to Snorri his followers practised cremation, and also buried hoards of gold in the earth in his honour. It seems to have been in the Migration and

Vendel periods that the cult of Odin reached its zenith in Sweden. In addition we find the male fertility deity with the boar as his symbol, also associated with warrior cults. The horse cult, which takes a prominent place in the religion of this period, seems to be associated with both these deities. As yet, however, the three main gods of the Viking Age, Odin, Freyr and Thor, have not become clearly defined.

CHAPTER VI

Powers of Asgard

The Æsir foregathered on Ida meadows, shrines and high fanes framed they of timber, forges erected, rich things they wrought, tongs devised, and tools they forged......

VǪLUSPÁ (Phillpott's translation).

VIKING GRAVES

THE LAST CHAPTER of paganism is that of the Viking Age, and it is from memories of this that our mythological literature has come, although its roots lie deeper still. The expansion of the Vikings took their religious traditions far beyond Scandinavia, and some of our evidence comes from this wider area. For reasons of space, however, we must be primarily concerned with Norway and Sweden, and to a lesser extent with Denmark, influenced by the Christian world more than the more northern territories. Pagan traditions carried to Iceland in the ninth and tenth centuries have left a rich literary harvest, but the archaeological evidence from there is limited, because of the abrupt physical break with ancient local tradition in Scandinavia. It was largely due to this that it was possible to introduce Christianity into Iceland almost painlessly in the year 1000.

There is no indication of a sudden break-through in funeral customs. Great variety is apparent in ways of disposing of the dead, and the impulse behind these obviously comes from previous periods. Only one practice, that of ship-funeral, spread with some vigour during the Viking Age as if there were some vital belief behind it.

Cremation and inhumation continued side by side, and there were no firm rules for procedure at the funeral. Cremation remained more popular in central Sweden, perhaps owing to the influence of the cult of Odin in this area. When in 1950 Ramskou surveyed the evidence for cremation in Denmark during the Viking Age, he could find no evidence of strong outside influences or dominant tradition affecting grave goods or mode of burial. In Lindholm in north Jutland, for instance, there were hundreds of cremation graves which were certainly pagan, and these were found to hold only simple grave goods such as ornaments, knives, whetstones and gaming-men, with an occasional dog, sheep or cow, but no signs of any established ritual.

Large burial mounds were still built for important people, while wooden burial chambers, with or without mounds, became fashionable for the rich. There are a number of these at the important trading centre of Birka in Sweden, many containing a horse or dog, while occasionally a woman would accompany the dead man. One grave held a woman with rich accessories, with a second woman lying in a twisted position, which might indicate that a servant was killed at her mistress' funeral. Archaeologists have disagreed as to how far fresh influences from abroad are responsible for these wooden chamber graves, as has already been indicated (see p. 107), and particular interest has been shown in graves of this type in Russia, in places where Swedish traders settled. It is hard to say which way the influence was moving, and possibly a new impetus for human sacrifice came into Scandinavia at this time, brought by travellers from the East.

Graves of the Viking Age were not in general very richly furnished. Fine swords and splendid weapons like the Mammen axe were sometimes buried with the dead, but a large proportion of the richest objects comes from hoards. Many swords have been recovered from rivers, so many indeed that Wilson has recently stressed the possibility that the custom of flinging weapons into the water was a form of ritual sacrifice continuing into this period. An exception to the general rule must however be made in the case of the great ship-burials, which are the subject of the next section.

The outstanding funeral symbol of the Vendel period and the Viking Age in Norway and Sweden is the ship of the dead, foreshadowed by tree coffins, ship outlines, and ships on memorial stones. Once adopted as the resting-place for the dead within the grave or on the pyre, the ship spread over the North with a rapidity comparable to the progress of the megalithic tomb. Ship-burials are found in Iceland, Brittany, England, Man and the Western Isles, as well as in Russia; indeed, wherever plunder and trade took Viking sea-captains in the heyday of their prosperity. Women too were laid in ships, and poorer folk used planks from boats as shelter for the dead, while outlines of ships in stones were made over cremation graves. If men were willing to undergo such trouble and expense, sacrificing good sea-going vessels for funeral ceremonies, it seems likely that the practice had definite symbolic meaning for them. Here at least it cannot be argued that they were imitating funeral practices of the Roman Empire or the Christian Church.

Occasionally in the sixth century in Norway ships were placed on pyres or buried. An inhumation boat-grave from Lødingen, Nordland, and a cremation boat-grave from Voss are claimed to be earlier than AD 600, and Shetelig gives other instances. However, elaborate ship burials began in Uppland in the seventh century, and were paralleled at about the same time in the kingdom of East Anglia in England. Besides the splendid royal burial at Sutton Hoo, there is an inhumation burial in a smaller boat in the same cemetery, with one end of the vessel apparently cut off to fit the grave. Further down the coast is the Snape ship-burial, and there are other possible examples from Ashby Dell and Catfield. These are burials of the mid seventh century, or possibly a little earlier, and a group of graves in the inhumation cemetery of Caister-on-Sea in Norfolk, where curved portions of boats were laid over the dead, belongs to about the same period. We know that pre-Christian East Anglia had close links with Uppland, for ancient treasures of Swedish workmanship were among the royal heirlooms at Sutton Hoo. In the Anglo-Saxon poem *Beowulf*, filled with heroic traditions from Denmark and Sweden, we have the most elaborate account of a ship-funeral in Northern literature. This tells how the ship of King Scyld was laden with weapons, jewels and national treasures, and the dead king lay by the mast with the royal standard beside him, while his ship was launched to sail to the unknown harbour from which he had come in infancy to rule the land.

In Uppland we have a group of ship cemeteries dating from the seventh century to the Viking Age. We know that the earlier Uppsala chiefs were cremated (see p. 107), but those who settled in Ulltuna, Vendel, Valsgärde and Tuna in Alsike were laid in ships, which were dragged ashore and lowered like mighty coffins into their graves. Although many of these graves were plundered or badly excavated, sufficient remains to give an impressive picture.

The first Vendel ship-burial was discovered by workmen in 1881, and when Arne published an account in 1927 there were at least twelve ship-graves known, extending over some 300 years in time. The pattern of burial was consistent, and in the earliest graves the dead man was placed in the stern, facing the prow, lying on some kind of bed. He had weapons and ornaments, sometimes helmet and coat of mail, while in the fore-part of the ship were ship's gear, drinking horns and cups, cauldrons and cooking equipment, gaming-boards and men, and sometimes food for the voyage. Animals slain at the funeral lay either in the boat or in the trench outside. Three or four horses were placed to starboard, facing the prow, and on the port side a cow or bull, several sheep, pigs and dogs, as well as occasional birds such as hawk, crane, geese and ducks. The same pattern was observed at Valsgärde, where the graves had not been disturbed, and were scientifically excavated. The dead man lay amidships, on mattress or cushions covered with cow-hide, under a tent or awning of birch bark, with his weapons beside him and the usual assortment of cooking gear, joints of meat, and animal carcases. The 15 ship-graves at Valsgärde showed exceptional conservatism in method of burial, since the the latest was about 1100 in date.

The ships had their prows pointing towards the water, and were loaded as if for a voyage. As Greta Arwidsson has pointed out, it was normal to put animals and stores in the fore-part, and for the crew's quarters to lie astern, while the captain's place would be near the centre. However, the pre-sence of horses and dogs, if not pigs and sheep, suggests definite sacrificial rites. The later Vendel graves show some difference in arrangement. In graves 9 and 14 the deceased sat up near the prow, and in the latter there was only one horse, saddled for riding, and two large dogs. In some of the later graves two horses were placed to face one another, in a manner recalling the pairs of horses on Gotland memorial stones.

Ship-funeral appears to have spread to Vestfold in Norway, where the splendid vessels of Oseberg and Gokstad have been preserved with their wooden contents by the blue clay in which they were buried, though both had been plundered long ago. They are dated to the second half of the ninth century, as is also the Tune ship, reasonably well preserved, and the Borre ship-burial, from which little survives. There were several im-pressive ship-burials further north, of which little is known: one at Rolvaøy was found in 1751, and said to be an unburnt ship holding cremated remains; others were reported from Karmøy (near Stavanger); Grønhaug, Myklebostad; Skei on Leka; and Hove on Løkta in north Helgeland. The only Danish ship-burial known, from Ladby in Funen, is dated about 900. Though the Vestfold ships faced the sea, the general rule in Norway, according to Shetelig, was to face

Plate 50

south. In the Vestfold graves the dead lay behind the mast, with much wooden furniture and equipment, including beds, sledges, a wagon, some elaborately carved posts, and animals slain to accompany the dead. There were about twelve horses and six dogs outside the Gokstad ship, and a peacock inside; about 15 horses, an ox and four dogs at Oseberg, many of them beheaded; and eleven horses and four dogs at Ladby.

A new feature in the Norwegian graves was a wooden burial chamber, shaped like a tent, built to hold the body behind the mast. At Tune the chamber was on a platform of piles protruding beyond the ship on either side, while at Karmøy stone walls were built on each side of the ship to support the chamber, which was roofed with birch bark. The Gokstad house was carefully made, with a ridge-pole, and the Oseberg one more crudely, with huge oak planks and boards filling the spaces between. It is interesting that such chambers were anticipated at Sutton Hoo in the seventh century, for the royal treasure was placed in a wooden house with a gabled roof built on top of the ship, about $17\frac{1}{2}$ feet long.

At Valsgärde men were buried in the ships, while women were cremated and placed in ordinary graves. Yet the Oseberg ship, richest of all the ship-graves in Scandinavia, was used for a woman. This was not an ocean-going vessel, but a pleasure ship for home waters, perhaps used on ceremonial occasions, and decorated with elaborate carving. One young and one elderly woman had been buried there, but the body of the younger had been removed except for a few bones when the grave was entered not long after the burial. Examination of the remains suggested that the old woman was an elderly attendant on a woman of high social standing. This hardly fits in with the theory advanced by several scholars that the burial was that of Queen Asa, widow of Gudrød and grandmother of Harald Fairhair, objections to which were clearly stated by Gjessing in 1942.

Graves of women buried in ships or boats have been found in Norway, for instance at Sørby, west of Sandefjord, where out of four ship-graves one was that of a woman. Examples are also known from Scotland and the Western Isles. Many women lay in boats at Kaupang, in the cemetery on the Bikholberg headland, where flat graves of men and women were closely packed together, and the dead buried in boats or portions of boats. One grave held a man and two women, interred at different times, and there were other cases of secondary burials. The boats varied from clumsy rowing boats to more elegant craft, and were sunk into the gravel in stone-lined graves, with a layer of stones above. Most of these graves were of the ninth century. Beside this we may set the impressive cemetery at Tuna in Västmanland, Sweden, where eight women had all been laid in ships about 20 feet in length, with a rich assortment of furnishing and wooden utensils. One elderly lady with plenty of possessions and clothes had the oars laid along the bulwark as if ready for the voyage. A rich Roman grave was found on the same site, where a woman with gold and silver objects and fine glass cups had been buried, and it is possible that this was an ancient cult centre connected with women.

It is hard to obtain reliable statistics about the cremation of ships, as rivets might easily escape notice in early excavations, and if parts of boats only were used, as at Kaupang, few traces would remain. Remains of boats have been recognized in cremation graves at Kaupang and Birka, and stone outlines in the shape of a boat were laid round cremation graves at Hojstrup and Lindholm Mark in Denmark and at Ølbor in Norway, while in the last case a boat had been burned on the funeral pyre. A grave of the late ninth or tenth century on the Ile de Groix in Brittany had over 800 rivets, indicating that a large ship had been burned. This had contained an adult man and a younger person, a dog and some birds, many shields, two swords, three axes and other weapons, as well as tools and orna-

ments of gold and silver. Additional evidence for ship cremation on a large scale comes from the records of an Arab traveller and diplomat, Ibn Fahlan, who visited Swedish settlers on
the Volga in the tenth century and described the cremation of
their chief in great detail. The man was first buried in the
ground, and later taken out, dressed in rich clothes and placed
on a bench covered with carpets and cushions within a tent on
the ship. Two horses, a dog and two cows were killed, and the
pieces thrown into the ship, then a cock and hen, and finally
a slave woman was put to death with long and elaborate ceremonial, and laid beside the dead man, after which the pyre
under the vessel was set alight. The general agreement with the
archaeological evidence is striking, and the narrative gives
some indication of the grim and dramatic ritual which may
have accompanied the great ship-funerals. It also raises the
interesting question, already posed with regard to the wooden
chamber tombs of the Viking period (see p. 112), of whether
the impetus for slaughter and cruel rites at the funeral of
important people had come into Sweden from South-East
Europe, by way of Russia.

There are many inconsistencies in the symbolism of ship-
funeral. The Ladby ship had the anchor stowed in the bows as
if for immediate departure, while the Oseberg ship was moored
to the land and weighed down by heavy stones. Some men lay
on the open deck, under a canopy, and others in heavy wooden
chambers clumsily erected on the ships. At Kiloran Bay in
Scotland and again at Hedeby the boat was inverted over the
dead, while at Hegge in south Trondhjem and in a grave in
Schleswig it was placed upside down on the roof of the grave
chamber. Parts only of a boat might be used, or rivets scattered
throughout the grave. Ibn Fahlan stated that poorer men
among the Rus had a small boat made specially for their cremation, while the chiefs would be buried in their own vessels.
We have seen, however, that local variations of this kind in-

evitably occur throughout the history of religious symbolism, and that when an important new symbol comes into use, it tends to combine with earlier ones, sometimes in what seems an illogical way. Thus it is hardly surprising to find the wooden house of the dead combined with ship-burial. In spite of such contradictions, the two most powerful motives behind the use of the ship would seem to be, first, to provide for the journey of the dead, and secondly, to use a symbol anciently associated with the powers of fertility. The fact that a ship formed one of the most valuable possessions of a chief meant, no doubt, that it possessed an added attraction as a status symbol, but this alone could hardly account for its use in important graves over so long a period.

The link between ship-funeral and the cult of the Vanir is implied, though never directly stated, in literary sources. The outstanding Vanir deities in Viking times were Freyr and Freyja, though there is no doubt that they were worshipped under many different names. Freyr is represented as the ancestor-founder of the Yngling kings of Sweden, and a ship formed one of his chief treasures. He was consistently associated with howe-burial, while his body was said to be preserved for some time after death, like that of the Rus chieftain. Njord, said to be the father of the Vanir pair, had close connections with ships and the sea, and many places called after him are found along the Norwegian coast and by lakes and rivers. There is a persistent tradition of a fertility deity who came in a ship over the sea as a child to form a royal dynasty, and it is he who is associated with ship-funeral in *Beowulf*. As with most literary sources written down long after the conversion, there are puzzling features in the *Beowulf* picture, for the king sent away in a ship was Scyld, said to be the first king of the Danes, and there is little evidence for ship-funeral in Denmark. However, in view of the many ship burials in East Anglia, the stress laid on this theme in an Anglo-Saxon poem is significant.

Connection with the Vanir could also explain the use of ship-burial for women. Those buried in ships at Tuna and Oseberg may have been priestesses of the Vanir. The wagon at Oseberg would have been well suited for religious processions like those associated with Nerthus and later with Freyr. The

Plate 51

terrifying carved heads (and perhaps also the strange objects thought to be rattles) could have been used to drive away hostile spirits, and would be in keeping with the more sinister side of the Vanir cult. The Oseberg ship held apples, hazel-nuts and seed as well as wheat for part of its cargo, and these are all recognized symbols of fertility, associated with the goddesses of plenty. It is even possible that the goddess, who was said to have visited the people of Denmark in a wagon, may have preferred in Norway to travel round the coast by ship.

In the Anglo-Saxon ship-graves there were no slain animals, and this might point to a retreat from full heathen rites in a partly converted country. Brøgger believed that the entering of the graves at Gokstad and Oseberg was not the work of tomb-robbers working in secret, but a deliberate act of open hostility against the evil magic of the howe-dwellers, made not long after burial took place. At Oseberg apparently purposeless damage was done to the ship itself, in particular to the curved serpent on the prow and to the splendid bed, which was hacked to pieces. This would be understandable were the mound the grave of a Vanir priestess, representing the evil goddess herself in the eyes of a community newly converted to Christianity. Although boat-burial is rare in Iceland, it was known there, and it may not be accidental that two men who according to the sagas were buried in boats were both priests of Freyr. While there are features in some of the burials in ships which point to Odin, god of the dead, and it would be rash to claim ship-funeral as exclusively connected with the Vanir, the evidence strongly suggests that its development on a large scale among chieftains in seventh-century Sweden was associated with their cult. Slaying of horses, pigs and horned animals is in keeping with worship of the Vanir, for although there is a consistent link between horse sacrifice and the sky-god, horses were undoubtedly sacred to Freyr, and were sacrificed to him. A ship-grave at Lamøya in the Kaupang area had marks of ploughing under its mound, another link with the fertility symbols of the Bronze Age (page 43 above).

The emphasis on the voyage of the dead is confirmed by such features as the stowing of the anchor, provision of oars, and the equipment of the vessels. The prows usually point towards sea or river, and in the apparently unsystematic burials at Kaupang this could have been the case, since the graves were on a headland with the sea on three sides. The boat may have served as a substitute for the wagon in graves of an earlier period, since in parts of Norway and Sweden it was the obvious form of travel, as in Ancient Egypt. Possibly the elaborate ship-funerals at Vendel were instituted by some family which believed that the dwelling of their gods lay across the sea, and developed the myth of the divine king coming to them over the waves.

An important feature of the Oseberg burial is a collection of tapestries from the burial chamber, restored by slow and painstaking work, results of which may be seen in the Viking Ship Hall at Byggdøy. Their full publication is eagerly awaited. The tapestries were in long narrow strips, probably meant to be placed round a hall or temple as a frieze. They show a vast number of figures, walking, riding, driving in small wagons, and standing in long ranks with upraised spears. Abstract motifs fill the spaces, and Hougen notes birds, swastikas and zig-zag lines among these, as on the bracteates, suggesting association with the sky-god. The impression is similar to that made by the figures on the helmets, the Gallehus horns and Gundestrup bowl, as well as by the rock carvings of the Bronze Age – that of a large number of worshipping figures and a few representatives of the gods or their special devotees. Rather than

Fig. 25a

scenes from myth or heroic tradition, it seems that here we have ceremonial processions grouped round various symbolic objects and dominating figures. A suggestive parallel from another age would be the figures round the frieze of the Parthenon.

Fig. 25 a, c

Among significant figures on the tapestry men in horned helmets, one holding crossed spears (and in the recent recon struction also a sword) can be made out, presumably associat ed with Odin; while it has been claimed that a tree with men hanging from it is also recognizable. There is a figure which Hougen calls a shieldmaid, wearing a boar headdress or mask, suggesting a link with the Vanir. Figures in animal masks and skins resemble those on the helmets and Gallehus horns. One wagon seems to hold two women, like the Oseberg ship itself, and another a man lying under a shield, which it has been suggested is a legendary king being carried into battle, although another possibility is that this is Freyr himself, borne in a wagon after death, as in the literary sources. Further dis cussion of the tapestries is not possible without access to the material, but they are an important reminder of the large part which weaving must have played in the dissemination of religious symbols and motifs, and they strengthen the argument for the religious significance of the Oseberg burial.

Fig. 25b

Literary sources show the Vanir worshipped along with Odin, and in the position which he sometimes appears to oc cupy as god of the sky, he might even figure as the husband of the earth goddess. Archaeological evidence in general implies that the deities were worshipped in groups, while certain places were sacred to one special cult. Oseberg and Tuna may have been cult centres of the Vanir, while the headland at Kaupang, where ship graves were crowded together, may also have pos sessed special sanctity. Hinsch notes that boat graves in Nor way tend to be set in groups around the large ship burials. Cemeteries like Vendel and Valsgärde seem to have been the graves of heads of families, or possibly leaders of warrior com

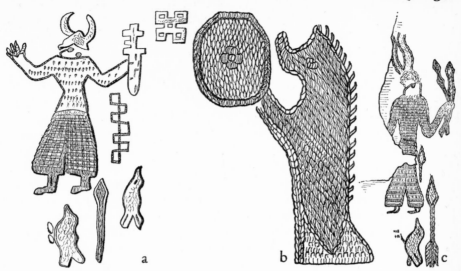

Fig. 25   Figures from the tapestries from the Oseberg ship, now in the Ship Museum, Byggdøe, Oslo (after Hougen)

munities who practised ship-funeral over a long period, whose traditions linked them with one special deity.

There is little evidence for any pictorial representation of the fertility gods and goddesses in the Viking Age. A striking exception is the small phallic figure in a pointed hat, found at Rällinge in Sweden, who is generally believed to be Freyr. This figure may have been used as an amulet, like the small Freyr-figures occasionally referred to in the literature, and he is modelled with skill and power, on a very different level from that of the little bearded men of the previous period. The goddess herself remains almost wholly elusive, and it may be that as a general rule the Vanir were depicted by means of their symbols, those of the boar, the horse, the wagon and the ship, which are closely linked with them in the literature.

Plate 59

123

THE HEROES OF ODIN

About the eighth century AD there was a new development in the memorial stones of Gotland. Many large ones were erected, in a characteristic 'mushroom' shape, with rounded top and straight sides widening towards the base, and some of these were covered with a bewildering series of small scenes, possibly illus/trating legends and myths. In their variety and detail, stones like those from Lärbro St Hammers, Buttle Ange, Hunninge and Ardre invite comparison with the Oseberg tapestries, but certain dominant motifs are clear.

Plates 53, 54

The ship still appears with its crew of warriors, and the accompanying figure is now a man on horseback, usually in the top panel. There seems little doubt that this is the dead man arriving in the Other World, as on Roman and Etruscan tombstones of a much earlier period, and he usually appears armed, in helmet and coat of mail, and is met by a female figure holding up a cup or drinking/horn. This suggests the recep/tion of the dead hero in Valhalla, as in tenth/century skaldic poems from Norway which describe the king arriving from the battlefield, and being met by the Valkyries who offer him wine. Occasionally the stones have interesting variants on this theme, and sometimes the rider has a hawk and dog with him, recalling the hawks and hunting dogs in some of the great ship burials.

Plate 52

Stone no. 3 from Lärbro St Hammers shows an eagle met by a woman with a cup, suggesting that here we have Odin in eagle form, either returning to Valhalla, or, as Lindqvist sug/gested, obtaining the mead of inspiration from the giant's daughter – a suitable theme perhaps for a poet's memorial. The eagle indeed appears on a number of stones, and a particularly interesting series of scenes are depicted on stone no. 1 from Lärbro Tängelgårda. First we see the eagle hovering over an empty saddle, while the rider lies on the ground. Then a seemingly dead man is carried on horseback, and beneath again

Plate 52

is the usual scene of welcome, with a woman greeting a rider and warriors brandishing rings. This stone appears to trace the progress of the dead warrior from the battlefield to Valhalla. Scenes of merry-making and feasting also appear, and one little group on a stone from Ardre has been interpreted by Oxenstierna as two men brandishing knives over the carcase of the pig reputed to be devoured each evening in Valhalla.

Two stones from Alskog Tjängvide and Ardre show a rider on a horse with eight legs. Another from Lärbro Tängelgårda shows the legs less distinctly, and Lindqvist thought it depicted a fence over which a four-legged horse is leaping, and suggested that the extra legs on the other stones had arisen from a mis-understanding of this scene; but the coincidence with literary tradition seems too striking to permit us to explain away the eight-legged horse, especially as he is also found in Siberia as the supernatural steed of the shaman. There is no sign of an eight-legged horse in earlier times, and this may be a relatively late conception of the god's steed, coming in by way of the Baltic. The rider of Sleipnir on these stones may be Odin, but is more probably the dead man riding on Odin's horse. I have elsewhere suggested that the basic idea behind the eight-legged horse is that of the bier carried by four men to the grave.

Plate 53

Plate 52

On the Lärbro St Hammers stone a warrior can be seen hanging from a tree, the traditional form of sacrifice to Odin, while an eagle and a flying figure which might be a valkyrie with a ring are seen above. Elsewhere, for instance on the Tjängvide stone, the flying figure appears to be guiding a spear in the air. A number of the stones have a motif which can roughly be described as a three-way knot, sometimes in the form of three triangles linked together, which is seen near the horse and the ship. This is a recognized weaving motif of some antiquity in Norway, known as the *valknut*. It is found also in the Oseberg ship, and on the tapestry from Oseberg, and ap-pears to have some special link with Odin.

Some stones clearly cover a wider range than the journey to the Other World, and their series of small pictures may be concerned with famous heroes who followed the cult of Odin. Many stories of Odin's heroes, such as Sigmund the Volsung, Hadding, and Harald Wartooth, survive in the literature, while many more must have been lost. When on the Gotland stones we find a woman standing between two armies, as at Lärbro St Hammers, or a house being defended against attack, as at Hunninge, it seems likely that such scenes have been inspired by heroic traditions of this kind. There is no evidence suggesting that the particular achievements of the men to whom the stones were raised were ever depicted there in their honour, although it is possible that scenes from the legendary past thought particularly appropriate to them may have been chosen, just as the poets used to glorify some new exploit by recounting a great tale of the past to which it might be compared.

Outside Gotland, pronounced interest was certainly felt in the story of one particular hero, Sigurd the Volsung. His dragon-killing exploit is shown in a series of scenes on two eleventh-century stones from Ramsund and Gök in Sweden, and other incidents from his cycle have been identified by some on stones from Ramsjö, Dräfle and Ockelbo, though these are more doubtful. The Ramsund stone, of which that from Gök is a crude imitation, shows the hero slaying the dragon and roasting its heart with his thumb in his mouth: this is because according to the story he burnt his thumb, sucked it, and obtained inspiration when the dragon's blood touched his tongue. The stone also shows two birds on a tree, who spoke to Sigurd and warned him of the treacherous smith, the dragon's brother; the smith is shown beheaded; and finally the hero's horse appears, laden with treasure. It is interesting to compare this stone with a number of stones from the British Isles, apparently slightly earlier than the Swedish examples, which show the same series of incidents, treated in a quite different style. Halton Cross in

Fig. 26

Fig. 26   Stone from Ramsund, Sweden, showing scenes from the Sigurd saga

Lancashire and three crosses from Jurby, Malew and Andreas Plate 56
on the Isle of Man all show the roasting of the heart, while the
other incidents from Ramsund are all to be found on one or
more of these stones. This parallelism suggests that the sculp-
tors were working in a fixed tradition, which dictated the choice
of scenes from the cycle, and its lasting popularity is proved by a
series of beautiful carvings of the same scenes on the portals of a
number of twelfth- and thirteenth-century stave churches from
Norway.

These memorials are Christian ones, and the continuing use
of scenes from the Volsung cycle in Christian times may have
been due to the fact that the families responsible for the Manx
and Halton crosses were able to claim descent from the royal
Volsung line. This might also account for a carved stone found
in the excavations at Winchester in 1965, showing a wolf
attacking a bound warrior who is biting the animal's tongue,
thought to be a scene from the story of Sigurd's father, Sigmund
the Volsung. The stone was found in the part of the Anglo-
Saxon cathedral for which Cnut, the Danish king, was re-

sponsible, and may be another example of renewed interest in the heroic past of which there is evidence at Jelling. Presum-ably in the pagan period such stones were raised by members of the warrior aristocracy who were worshippers of Odin.

Another of the Manx crosses, at Ramsey, has a scene even more closely connected with pagan myth, showing Loki kil-ling the otter with a stone, an incident which has been linked by Snorri in the Prose Edda with the story of Sigurd and the dragon. Another, from Andreas, has a bound figure surround-ed by snakes, to which there are a number of Scandinavian parallels. It has usually been thought to illustrate the death of Gunnar, Sigurd's brother-in-law, in a snake pit, where he was placed by King Atli as an act of revenge. In some medieval Scandinavian carvings the bound man is playing a harp with his feet, in accordance with one of the literary versions of the story; but on Andreas Cross, and again on the Oseberg wagon and on three of the Gotland stones, the man among the snakes has no harp. I think it possible that in these earlier carvings we have a pagan tradition of a sacrificial death among snakes, like that associated with Ragnar Lothbrok, the legendary hero who slew a dragon and whose sons are said to have conquered England. Nordland has argued for a Christian origin for this serpent motif, based on the idea of serpents as creatures of the tomb, but its appearance at Oseberg and in Gotland suggests that once again a vigorous pre-Christian tradition in the North has merged with Christian symbolism from outside.

Another group of stones appears to preserve memories of the last battle of gods and monsters at Ragnarok, a theme closely associated with Odin. In Cumberland someone must have been deeply interested in the old pagan subjects, for they are used very effectively in a number of monuments of the tenth and eleventh centuries. Panels on the cross at Gosforth show battles with monsters, and the bound Loki; two impressive hogbacks in the church, badly preserved and in a position

Plate 57

Plate 55

which makes it difficult to examine them, show battles against serpents and an encounter between two armies. Not far away, at Heysham, there is another hogback with scenes claimed to represent Ragnarok, for which no convincing Christian inter-pretation has been found, and there are one or two possible Ragnarok scenes on the Manx crosses.

There seems no doubt that on the Gosforth cross scenes from pagan tradition have been used to express a Christian belief in the triumph of Christ over the forces of evil and darkness. While the difficulties of exact dating and interpretation of these carvings are considerable, it is important to recognize the amount of evidence available on them. These, like the series of Gotland stones, may well be a late example of a tradition once forming part of the cult of Odin, the representation of famous heroes and of the last battle between gods and monsters.

There is evidence for a similar tradition in Scandinavia also. The Swedish stone from Altuna (see p. 132) has a man on horseback faced by a tall figure behind a gate, perhaps another representation of the dead arriving in the Other World. A tenth-century stone from Alstad in Norway has been interpreted by Lis Jacobsen as showing Sigurd's murderers riding home from the wood; however, in view of the eagle at the top and the parallel examples of riders with dogs on the Gotland stones, this again may be a variant on the same theme. The Swedish stone from Sparlösa, Västergotland, has a building at the top, a ship and a warrior on horseback, and again fits into the same pattern. The wide distribution of such motifs may well be due to the popularity of tapestries like those from Oseberg, which could travel over the sea and link Gotland with Man; nor must the importance of woodcarving as another medium be forgotten. Such mythical and symbolic scenes appear to have formed an important by-product of the cult of the god of battle and the dead. Those connected with the cult of Thor will be discussed separately (see pp. 132-4).

Plate 65

In the great ship-burials, a merger seems to have taken place between the cults of Odin and the Vanir, in cases where a warrior chief was laid in his ship with weapons, horses and dogs. There seems to have been little attempt to portray the god himself. Just as symbols often represented the Vanir, so the warrior seems to have been the chief representative of Odin's cult. The male emissary of Vendel times is now replaced by a woman who greets the dead and sometimes guides the spear. These figures are not confined to the carved stones, but are also found in the form of small silver figures in Swedish graves.

Plate 62
Plate 58

Figures of a warrior on horseback and one example of a man in a robe and horned headdress of the type associated with Odin in Vendel times have also been found. These little figures, a number of which come from graves in Birka, are interesting and significant. There is also one set of very tiny charms in the National Museum at Stockholm, which includes a horse and some weapons, and might be associated with Odin's cult, intended to bring good luck in battle.

Plate 63

The new emphasis laid on the woman who welcomes war-riors to the realm of the gods marks a change in the conception of the valkyries, and is confirmed by descriptions in the litera-ture. The earlier conception of fierce female spirits attending the war-god, and of a male figure guiding the spear in battle, now seems to have been replaced by a different picture, and it is possible that this came into Scandinavia from the East, by way of Gotland.

The growing influence of Christian traditions makes it hard to unravel the tangle of beliefs and practices surrounding Odin the All-Father, worker of magic and god of the dead. There must have been a rich esoteric complex of magic and ritual in funeral ceremonial, to which the cults of Odin and the Vanir contributed. This is confirmed by a long runic inscription from

Plate 66

Eggjum in Sogn, found in 1917, and believed to be a memorial to a dead man, although in the grave beneath nothing was

130

found but a knife and strike-a-light (objects which may have some relevance in view of the first line of the inscription). Between the runes there is a bold outline of a horse's head, suggesting a link with the memorial stones and with the steed of Odin. Some have dated the inscription to about 800, but Gerd Höst, in his detailed study of 1960, puts it in the seventh century. However, it seems right to mention it here as part of the evidence relating to Odin, for he claims to find in it a reference to Odin himself as *Héráss*, the God of Hosts. Until now the first reading by Magnus Olsen has been accepted with a few minor amendments; he took the stone to commemorate a man named Ormarr, whose name was indicated by two riddling statements, the answers to which were *ormr*, serpent, and *arni*, eagle. Höst however follows Nordén in rejecting this, and gives a translation of the runes running roughly as follows:

This stone is not taken in sunlight, nor cut with knife. No one shall uncover...while the moon is waning, and the wandering (bewitched?) man shall work no evil upon it.
The man smeared this stone with magical seawater (blood?) and with it scraped the wedges of the upper mast.
In what form comes *Héráss* (Odin) to the land of the Goths (land of men?)?
As a fish swimming out of...the river of the body, as a bird shrieking...
This is the work of.........(followed by name of rune-maker).

There are many controversial points in this rendering, and the detailed arguments supporting it must be followed in the work of Höst and his predecessors. It is, however, worth noting the main implications of this inscription. There is insistence on rites and taboos, presumably connected with burial, a reference to a ship, and, according to this new interpretation, a conception of the god travelling in the spirit world in the shape of fish

131

and bird (presumably eagle). Höst believes that the reason for this is to enable Odin to lead the dead man to his realm, and this is an attractive suggestion, since it offers links with the eagles on the Gotland and Swedish stones, and reminds us of the fish on the Kivik slab. It is in accordance with the shamanistic powers which Odin possesses in the Eddic literature, and serves to remind us how much dark magic may have been associated with him in the way of funeral ritual.

THE GOD OF THE HAMMER

The cults of Odin and the Vanir were already flourishing in Vendel times, but that of Thor seems not to have become dominant until the Viking period, and to have reached its height in the tenth and eleventh centuries, leaving a vivid mark on the surviving literature. This cult has also inspired some carved memorial stones of the Viking Age.

The myth concerning Thor which particularly impressed itself on the imagination of the poets is his struggle with the World Serpent, when he pulled it out of the sea and saved the world from destruction only by smiting it down with his hammer. One of several poems of the tenth century concerned with this exploit claims to be describing a carving in an Icelandic hall, and a small group of stones from widely separated regions have survived which show Thor fishing for the monster.

Plate 65

One of the best-known of these is that from Altuna in Sweden, where the god appears alone in a boat, with hammer raised in his right hand and his foot breaking through the boat as he braces himself against the sea-bed. Serpent and ox-head bait can be clearly distinguished.

Fig. 27

Another stone, from Hørdum Ty in Denmark, although incomplete, must be concerned with the same theme, as the god with feet breaking through the boat and part of the serpent can be seen. Other possible examples have been suggested:

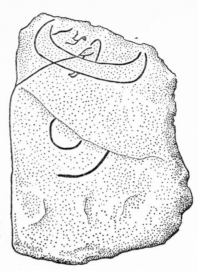

*Fig. 27   Stone from Hørdum Ty, Den-
mark, showing Thor fishing for the monster (after Brøndsted)*

one is on the Ardre stone from Gotland, where two figures in a   Plate 53
boat might be Thor and Hymir the giant, as in the account of
the fishing in *Hymiskviða*. Finally, in a stone built into the wall
of the Gosforth church in Cumberland, two figures appear in a   Plate 64
boat, one with upraised hand as on the Altuna stone, though
the surface is too worn to make out the hammer. The ox-head
is fairly clear, and round it swim several fish, while the serpent
may be represented by the twisted coil above the boat. It is not
known whether this stone originally formed part of a pagan or
Christian memorial, but the figure above suggests the fettered
wolf.

The Ardre stone might possibly show other incidents from
the story, as a bearded figure approaching an animal in an   Plate 53
enclosure can be made out, and seen again walking with a
burden on his back; these scenes might represent the fetching of
the ox's head from the giant's herd. A bearded man is also
seen beside a many-headed figure, and it has been suggested
that this illustrates the lost myth of Thor's battle with a many-

133

headed giant. It is possible that this stone was mainly devoted to the adventures of Thor, but unfortunately the other scenes have not been identified.

The popularity of Thor's fishing adventure is explicable by the fact that this is a universal myth, fitting into the world pattern of the struggle between the sky-god and the monster of the deep, the serpent or dragon, in order to save the world from destruction. It must have occupied as central a position in Thor's cult as did the riding to the Other World in that of Odin.

We have no surviving picture of Thor in his wagon drawn by goats, as described in the literature. There is however a small bronze figure, about 7 cm. high, from Akureyri in

Plate 60

northern Iceland, which might well be a miniature copy of the images of the god seated in pagan temples. The little man wears a conical hat, like the supposed image of Freyr (see p. 123), and he is resting his chin on a cross-shaped object held in his hands, which appears to be an ornamental hammer; indeed on closer inspection this seems to be growing out of his beard. The identification of the beard of the god with the hammer causing the lightning is consistent with the emphasis in the literature on the red beard of Thor, the shaking of which was said to cause storms. Another possible Thor, this time carved in bone, is a small man from Lund, who is also holding

Plate 61

his beard, this time twisted into a kind of plait. Gjærder has suggested that the pattern of circles on the back of his chair represents a hammer on a loop, like that shown on memorial stones.

There is certainly no doubt of the popularity of the hammer symbol in the last period of paganism, for many hammer amulets survive from all parts of Scandinavia and places where the Vikings settled. Moreover, it is clearly depicted on memorial stones of the tenth century and later. In Denmark it is shown on four runic stones from Læborg, Spentrup, Gard-

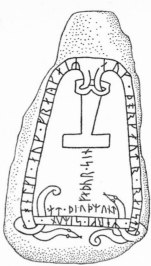

Fig. 28 Runic stone from Stenkista, Söderman-land, Sweden, showing Thor's hammer

stanga and Karlevi respectively, where it forms an introduc-tion to the runes, like the cross on Christian runic stones; a fifth example, from Hanning, is as late as the twelfth century in date. On some stones from Södermanland in Sweden the hammer hangs from the loop forming the band on which the runes are carved, and on one of these, from Åby, the hammer touches a bearded face as if the beard rested upon it, as in the case of the Icelandic figure. Some of the Danish inscriptions call on Thor to 'hallow this memorial', or to 'hallow these runes', while one particularly interesting inscription from Lundbø, Bratsberg, in Norway, calls on the god to 'take to yourself the body lying beneath this stone'. Clearly the hammer was regarded as some kind of protection for the dead in the grave, perhaps even as a symbol of immortality, and once more the deliberate parallel with the Christian cross is apparent.

Similarly the little metal hammers of iron, bronze and silver, so popular in the late Viking Age, must have been inspired in part by the cross worn by Christians. A mould in the National

Fig. 28

Museum at Copenhagen shows that hammers and crosses could be made side by side to satisfy the varying tastes of customers. Hammer amulets however were known in pagan times, for several small examples have survived from Kentish cemeteries of the sixth or seventh centuries, and there must be a link between the hammers and the little axe amulets (many of these virtually indistinguishable from hammers) which are found all over the Baltic region, dating from the early Viking period and from much earlier times, as Paulsen shows in his invaluable detailed study of axe and cross. Sets of tiny hammers of iron on a ring are found in graves at Birka, and in one Uppland cemetery, that of Lilla Frescati excavated in 1911, they occurred in six out of seven mounds holding cremation burials.

Plate 67   The elaborate little amulets in bronze and silver from the tenth century are more complex symbols. Some have faces with round, staring eyes, and sometimes also the beak of a bird of prey, evidently influenced by the familiar motif of the eagle. It seems likely that these were intended to portray the terrible fiery eyes of the god of the lightning, emphasized in the literature, while it is noticeable that the hammer-head sometimes takes the place of a beard. Some of the hammers have elaborate

Plate 67   chains, ending in dragon-heads, biting on to the ring which holds the hammer, and these probably symbolize the World Serpent, Thor's adversary. The ring itself may be a reminder of the sacred ring of Thor, the symbol of law and order, said to be kept in his temples, on which oaths were sworn. There are also patterns of circles and criss-cross lines on the hammers, suggesting rain and lightning.

Such hammers are mostly found in hoards rather than graves. Some of the hoards may have been votive offerings to Thor, or treasures hidden by the owners of his temple; Paulsen notes that one hoard from Torslev, Jutland, contains a silver bowl with a hammer sign on the underside, which might have been used in

Thor's worship, and richly decorated hammer amulets may have been intended to be worn by Thor's priest, in imitation of a cross. Another possible reason for the inclusion of the hammer, however, might be the belief that it gave protection against thieves.

Some of the superbly decorated axes of the Viking Age may have been ritual weapons, or possibly special marks of rank associated with Thor, the upholder of the established order. The position of such axes in tenth-century graves sometimes implies something of this kind. At the wooden chamber tomb of Mammen near Viborg, in Denmark, discovered in 1869, the dead man, richly clothed, lay on a down cushion with two axes at his feet. One axe was of plain iron, but the other was splendidly decorated with gold and silver inlay, and bore a bearded face and some swastika-like figures as part of its decoration. Another decorated axe from Skensta, Uppland, has what seems to be a form of the hammer sign on it. Many elaborate axes of this kind are found in the grave-mounds of Denmark, Sweden, Finland and north Russia.

The axe symbol remained of importance from the earliest times to the end of the pagan period, while after the conversion the figure of Olaf the Holy with an axe in his hand obviously took over from the pagan god. In the late Viking Age, the throwing-hammer on a cord or chain seems to have superseded the axe as the weapon of the sky-god, and Thor's hammer is described in this way in the literature. Undoubtedly Thor took over many of the attributes of the ancient sky-god, and seems to have borrowed some from Odin. The swastika, for instance, appears to have been increasingly used as his symbol, probably on account of its resemblance to the hammer. This survived in Iceland as a magic sign known as *tórshamarr*, and in the last century figured in spells in which a drawing of a pair of eyes was used in association with a hammer and a spike. The swastika and also the staring eyes were familiar motifs in both the

Vendel and the Viking period, and seem to have been associated with the sky-god, and so ultimately with Thor. The province of Thor must to some extent have overlapped with that of Odin, because both were connected with the sky and with the dead, and both could be associated with cremation. In the eleventh century Adam of Bremen tells us that the Swedes were sacrificing to Thor as a fertility deity, so that here there may also have been encroachment on the powers of the Vanir. Certainly by the close of the pagan period he was looked on as chief adversary of Christ, and the most popular god among the western Vikings.

THE HOLY PLACES

The evidence of Scandinavian place names shows how many local sites were dedicated to a god or goddess, so that they must in some sense have been holy ground. Some deities of which little trace has survived in the written sources, such as Ull and Njord, have inspired many place names, dating to a period before the Viking Age. This evidence is important for the picture which it gives of the extent of early cults, and it serves also as a reminder of how virtually impossible it is to fit names to the early figures of the gods which survive from the Early Iron Age, since it seems that the god of the sky and the goddess of fertility must have been worshipped locally under many different designations.

It has been claimed also that place names can tell us something about temple sites. In Norway more than 85 farms have names formed from *hof*, which is thought by some to indicate the existence of a temple building, the larger of these replaced by churches and the smaller by chapels-at-ease. In Iceland a more deliberate plan was worked out by the settlers, and the *hof* areas appear to have been roughly equal in size; though whether these names indicate that a building was ever erected for the worship of the gods is doubtful. After detailed examination of the literary and archaeological evidence, Olaf Olsen has come to the conclusion that in general the ordinary farm buildings were used when people from the district gathered for sacrifices and feasting, and that ceremonies for the most part took place out of doors. There were certainly many sacred places, some going back to very early times, where sacrifices were made and which were associated with various deities.

We have indeed very little definite evidence about temple buildings, and most of the traditions in Iceland about local temples at *hof* sites appear to have originated in the nineteenth century. One large building at Hofstaðir, near Lake Mývatn in northern Iceland, was excavated in 1908, and hailed with much enthusiasm as a pagan temple, its plan appearing in most works on Viking religion. The building was a long, boat-shaped hall, like those at Trelleborg, with pillars separating the central part from aisles on either side. There were long fires down the centre, and additional hearths at either end, a raised section for seats facing the fires, and additional seats facing into the side aisles. The hall would have seated about 150 men, and there was stabling for the same number of horses in outbuildings. It was claimed that this hall was separate from the original farm site, and a number of paths can be traced leading to it from many directions. It must have served for some kind of communal gathering for the district, and was certainly used for feasting, since a large number of bones of sheep, oxen, goats, pigs and horses, as well as fish-bones of haddock, were found there.

Such a building may well have been used for the great feasts held at yule and autumn, when many cattle and horses were sacrificed and the blood offered to the gods, according to accounts in the literature. Nothing however marks out the hall as a sacred building, and it illustrates the difficulties which beset the archaeologist who tries to find the site of a heathen temple. At one end of the hall, divided from it by an unbroken wall, was an annexe with its own door. This building was nearly square, and the excavator thought he found traces of rounded corners, and compared it to the apse of a church. It was suggested that worshippers in the hall might have glimpsed the figures of gods in the apse through a window in the wall, while only the priest was allowed to enter through the outside door. This however is no more than surmise, and the building may have been a storeroom. Olsen lays more weight on the fact that an oval ridge was found in the earth near one of the doors at the front of the hall, and in this bones, burnt stones and ash were found. It seems most unlikely for a refuse pit to be placed in this position, and he suggests that it was used for ritual preparation of the sacrificed animals when a large gathering met for the ceremonial feast. It seems probable that the *hof* farms were those possessing a large hall suitable for such assemblies, but that the hall was not reserved for these occasions, being probably occupied by the people of the farm in the normal way.

Descriptions in the literature imply that small wooden buildings served as shrines for the gods. This probably explains the use of the word *horgr* as distinct from *hof*. The *horgr* was certainly a place of sacrifice, often associated with the goddesses of fertility in the poetry. Its earlier form may have been a ring of stones, such as that surrounding the megalithic tombs and placed round sacred objects like the wooden man from Broddenbjerg. We have no proof that this developed into a small rectangular building, or that various constructions of this type excavated in Iceland were ever pagan shrines.

Plate 68

Nevertheless a possible clue to the type of temple used in the late Viking period is offered by the medieval stave churches of wood, surviving from the twelfth and thirteenth centuries in Norway. These are not very large, but high, dark and impressive within, with a lofty roof rising in a number of gables. The earliest type is thought to be that with four main pillars supporting the central part of the building, ornamented with intricate carving of twisted creatures on portals and decorative panels, and vigorous carved heads on the pillars round the walls. The pagoda-like series of roofs, rising one above the other and ending in dragon-heads like the figure-heads of ships, gives a strangely oriental effect. The impression of the whole strongly suggests a link with the pagan conception of the World Tree joining earth and heaven, while the creatures writhing in unending conflict, to be found at Urnes and Hopperstad, and recalling the Tree which was continually destroyed and renewed, strengthens this impression. The fantastic heads with stylized 'beards' below call to mind the images of Thor said to be carved on pillars of pagan temples in Norway and sometimes carried to Iceland by early settlers, to bring the sanctity of the holy places into the new land. The most elaborate stave churches, those at Urnes, Hopperstad, Borgund and Gol, give some indication of the strangeness and dignity which may have characterized the lost temples of the gods.

Plate 68

Such temples – always assuming that they existed – would presumably have been products of the late Viking Age. The special characteristics of the stave churches were established in Norway by the second half of the eleventh century, and might have been taken over from pagan temples. Olsen suggests that these high wooden buildings with their square central section under the loftiest part of the roof would be admirably planned for the placing of images of the gods surrounded by carved pillars. He thinks that they may have developed out of a small roof supported on four posts, set up as a shelter for idols out in the open air. The example of Christian churches no doubt led the Scandinavians to construct larger and richer houses for their gods, but it is significant that they seem to have made no attempt to imitate English examples when they began to build their wooden churches, presumably because a native tradition had already been established and was readily adaptable for Christian worship.

It seems unlikely however that there were many pagan sanc/ tuaries of this kind, since unremitting search under early Danish churches has so far failed to bring to light remains of early temples, except possibly at Jelling. Nor have remains been found of the temples of Thor and Freyr said to stand in central Norway. All the same the famous temple at Uppsala must have stood roughly where the medieval church still stands, near the sacred grove and the royal burial mounds (see p. 107). Lindqvist excavated here in 1926, and claimed to have discovered the plan of a larger thirteenth/century church beneath the present one, and also traces of a wooden building earlier still. He assumed from the small number of recognizable post/holes that this building was almost square, and that it lay under the nave of the present church and extended beyond it on the north side; but the evidence is insufficient to determine whether this was an early wooden church or a pagan temple, and reconstructions of the heathen temple based on it have not been generally accepted.

Fig. 29

West of the church stand a few ash trees, and it is thought that this was the place of the sacred grove, described in Adam of Bremen's eleventh/century account of Uppsala. Here it is claimed that an old man who visited the temple not long before remembered seeing animal and human sacrifices hanging from the trees. The sites of two wells are known, and one or other of them may have been that in which it was reputed that victims were drowned. According to Adam the temple stood in a plain, surrounded by mounds 'like a theatre', and indeed the line of burial mounds would have provided convenient seating for spectators watching ceremonies carried out in the grove. Nothing is said about the building itself except that over its roof there ran a golden chain, visible to those who approach/ ed. Lindqvist suggested that the carved frieze on a roof of the

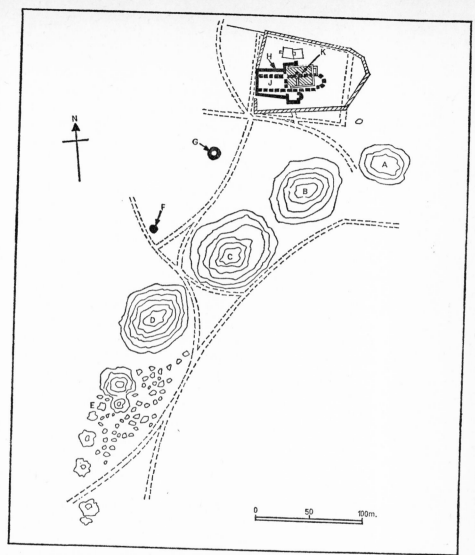

Fig. 29 Plan of mounds and church at Old Uppsala, Sweden, showing previous plans of the church revealed by excavation. A Domar bögen. B East Mound (Odin's Howe). C Middle Mound (Freyr's Howe). D West Mound (Thor's Howe). E Area of small mounds. F Well (Minnurs brunn). G Well (Urdals brunn). H Plan of cathedral church. J Existing church. K Suggested plan of temple

stave-church type, tipped with gold, would give the effect of such a chain. This, like the golden dome of the Eastern Ortho-dox churches, which symbolizes heaven, might have represent-ed the gleaming houses of the gods beyond the earth, of which the Edda poems tell.

The sanctity of the site at Uppsala was presumably estab-lished long before any temple was built, by the existence of the royal graves and possibly also the grove and the wells. A similar sanctuary appears to have existed at Leire, the modern Roskilde in Denmark, where Danish kings were buried, and Thietmar of Merseburg records great sacrifices there every nine years. When Gorm the Old gained independence again for Denmark about 940, after a period of Swedish overlordship, one of his first acts was to plan a holy place at Jelling, where his palace stood. A good deal is known about the history of this site, as the result of excavations by Einar Dyggve between 1941 and 1955.

Fig. 30

Gorm chose for his holy place a site where a line of Bronze Age tumuli already stood. With one of these as the base, he constructed a large triangular enclosure formed of standing stones over 6 feet high, in front of the ancient mound. Dyggve believes that this deliberate use of stones in the manner of the megalithic builders was a conscious act of antiquarianism on the part of King Gorm, an enthusiasm for the heroic past characteristic of the Viking Age. Gorm then built a new mound on top of the Bronze Age barrow, the present north mound at Jelling. It held a burial chamber, probably left open to serve as a tomb for the king himself and his queen Tyra, with the smaller runic stone found at Jelling set on top as a memorial. In 1821 a man accidentally found his way into this chamber, but by then the bodies had been removed, and only two silver cups, some painted wood and a chest were left inside. The chamber was further excavated and restored in 1861, and again investigated by Dyggve in 1942.

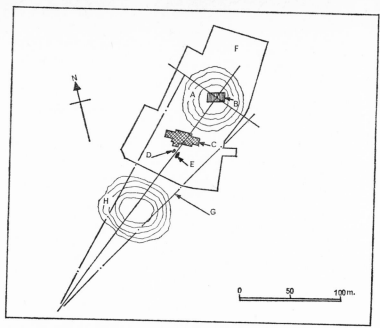

*Fig. 30   Plan of sanctuary at Jelling, Denmark, showing lines of bauta stones as recon-
structed by Dyggve. A Northern mound. B Burial chamber. C Church. D Small runestone. E Great runestone. F Churchyard. G Lines of bauta stones. H Southern mound*

Dyggve also excavated the second mound. This lay to the
south, over the apex of the triangle. It had been built with a
flat top, and a rectangular building had stood on its summit,
supported by posts and solid blocks of wood. Within the
mound there was no burial chamber, but only a strange erection of wood, which appeared to be a symbolic house of the
dead. It was either roofless or had a roof of perishable material,
while the sides were packed round with turf and the building
could never have supported itself. This construction had been
left exposed to the air for some time and then covered by the
mound. The southern mound was built about 40 years after

the northern one, and was presumably the work of Gorm's son Harald while he was still pagan, perhaps destined for his own tomb.

When he was converted to Christianity, Harald must have built the first church, at the point where the present one stands, across the central axial line of the sanctuary. Dyggve found the clay floor of an earlier building under the existing church, and the great stone which must have served for an altar had been left beneath the new floor; this was a block of fine dark granite shot with reddish garnet, and might have been taken over from the pagan site. Below the clay floor was another which had belonged to a wooden structure, the posts of which had been pulled out when the building was abandoned after about 30 years of use. Dyggve believed this to have been Gorm's heathen temple. The church with the clay floor had been of the stave type, although its posts were placed in the earth and not on a sill, as in the Norwegian examples. This in turn had been burnt down, and the present Romanesque church built in its place. When Harald was converted, he seems to have moved the bodies of his parents from the northern mound for Christian burial, pulled down the temple, overturned the megaliths, and erected his new church in the sanctuary, which became a Christian graveyard. He set up the great runic stone with its proud message and the figure of Christ upon it, perhaps as a substitute for the burial mound and the stone which would have been his pagan memorial.

Thus at Jelling we have a sanctuary of the tenth century, planned and constructed with considerable skill, and modelled on funeral monuments of the remote past. Dyggve at first claimed to have found two other sites of the Viking Age where tumuli were enclosed in this way, but further investigation has disproved this, and it seems that Gorm may have been an innovator. Some doubt has also been cast on the identification of the wooden building as Gorm's temple, since it may possibly have been the first of three Christian churches, but the main history of the sanctuary remains clear.

At the end of the pagan period, then, we find the ancient symbols, the great standing stones, the house of the dead within the mound, and the holy place where the king was buried, still accepted, and set up once more in a last stand against the encroachments of the new religion.

The last phase of paganism was in many ways a fairly vigorous one. The gods and goddesses of fertility continued to be worshipped, especially in the great ship-burials with their plentiful sacrifices, while the holy places were still held in reverence. Odin's cult was commemorated by carved stones, raised by the proud descendants of past heroes. Thor the hammer-god took to himself the ancient powers and symbols of the god of the sky. The houses of the gods seem to have increased in splendour and impressiveness. There was conscious rivalry with the Christian Church, and deliberate archaism, which expressed itself also in outbursts of mythological poetry and the re-chronicling of old tales. The presentiment that the world was ending as the year 1000 drew near was not after all wholly misleading in Northern Europe, for now the pagan world, which since Neolithic times had followed certain religious patterns, was drawing to its close. Although it is true that many of its practices, symbols and themes can still be traced in Christian times, nevertheless the break was an abrupt one, and a process which began with the wandering hunters and the first farmers may now be said to be over.

We have seen in the course of this survey how firmly established certain conceptions and motifs have been in the North, so that even when new influences came in from outside, lending a new emphasis or introducing different types of worship, there was a fixed tendency to return to the pattern which already existed in the Bronze Age. At the same time new inspirations kept alive the pagan faith, still coming in, it would seem, from the pagan East even when Christianity was firmly established in Western and Central Europe. When however the tendency, as in King Gorm's sanctuary at Jelling, seems to be to look back to the remote past rather than to move forwards, it is a sign that the end is drawing near.

The coming of an organized monotheistic religion, with its roots in the Near East, developed over the centuries by scholars and philosophers, meant a complete reshaping of man's attitude towards the supernatural. The priests of the new faith would brook no rivalry, and the old gods were banished. Moreover, with Christianity we enter into the epoch of the written word, and pass on into the new civilization of the Christian Middle Ages. The work of the northern gods was done.

Select Bibliography

General

ARCHAEOLOGY: Brøndsted (1957–9); Hagen (1967); Klindt-Jensen (1957); Stenberger (1962).
RELIGION: Eliade (1958); de Vries (1956) – both with helpful bibliographies; Grønbech (1931).

CHAPTER I

PRIMITIVE RELIGION: Campbell (1960); James (1957) – both with helpful bibliographies; Bowra (1962); Frobenius (1923); Schmidt (1912–55); Van der Post (1959).
SHAMANISM: Eliade (1964).
ROCK CARVINGS: *Art of the World* (1961); Gjessing (1932, 1945); Hagen (1965); Hallstrom (1960); Kuhn (1952).
EARLY MAN IN DENMARK: Møhl-Hansen (1954).
CARVED FIGURES: Mathiassen (1959).

CHAPTER II

MEGALITHIC TOMBS: Bagge and Kaelas (1950); Childe (1962); Daniel (1963); Evans (1959); Hawkes (1940); Kaelas (1955); Levy (1948).
MOTHER GODDESS: Crawford (1957); James (1959).
VOTIVE OFFERINGS: Becker (1962); Björn (1927).
DOUBLE FUNERAL: Hertz (1960).

CHAPTER III

FUNERAL CUSTOMS: Fox (1959); Gjessing (1942); Grinsell (1941).
TREE COFFINS: Childe (1949); Hawkes (1940).
KIVIK GRAVE: Grinsell (1942).
ROCK CARVINGS: B. Almgren (1962); O. Almgren (1927); Althin (1945); Gelling and Davidson (in the press).

WAGONS: Bing-Bergen (1934); Drescher (1962); Hagen (1955); Schmid (1934).
LURER: Broholm (1949).
HELMETS: Norling-Christiansen (1946).
ORNAMENT: Knight (1932); Sprockhoff (1954, 1955).
HUMAN FIGURES: Drjupedal and Broholm (1952); Lindqvist (1942); Rosenberg (1929).
VOTIVE FINDS: Ingstad (1961).

CHAPTER IV
BOG-FINDS: Andersen (1951); Glob (1965); Jankuhn (1936); Rosenberg (1937); Ørsnes (1963, 1964).
CELTIC PEOPLES: Powell (1958) – with extensive bibliography.
CELTIC RELIGION: Lambrechts (1942); Sjœstedt (1949).
RITUAL OBJECTS: Klindt-Jensen (1949, 1960).
ALAISIAGAE: Bosanquet (1922).

CHAPTER V
BRACTEATES: Mackeprang (1952).
GULDGUBBER: Grieg (1954); Nordén (1939).
GALLEHUS HORNS: Brøndsted (1954); Oxenstierna (1956).
DANCERS: Beck (1964); S. Hawkes and Davidson (1965); Holmqvist (1960).
HUMAN FIGURES: Grieg (1954); Jankuhn (1958); Mackeprang (1935)
FRØIHOV: M. Olsen (1914–24).
GOTLAND STONES: Lindqvist (1941–42, 1962).
SÆTRANG GRAVE: Slomann (1959).
UPPSALA MOUNDS: Lindqvist (1936).
THE SEAT ON THE HOWE: Lehman (1910); Olrik (1909); Taringer (1934).
HORSE CULT: Gjessing (1943); Klindt-Jensen (1957); Lid (1957).

CHAPTER VI
ARCHAEOLOGY: Arbman (1961); Brøndsted (1960); Oxenstierna (1965); Shetelig (1940–54).
RELIGION: Davidson (1964); Turville-Petre (1964).

FUNERAL CUSTOMS: Arbman (1940) Arne (1931); Brøndsted (1936); Ramskou (1950).

VENDEL CEMETERY: Stolpe and Arne (1927).

VALSGÄRDE CEMETERY: Arwidsson (1942, 1954).

ANGLO-SAXON SHIP-BURIALS: Bruce-Mitford (1949, 1952, 1964); Green (1963).

BRITTANY SHIP-BURIAL: Chatellier (1908).

SHIP-BURIAL: Brøgger (1945); Hinsch (1946); Nicolaysen (1882); Shetelig (1917); Stolpe (1895).

TUNA: Stenberger (1956).

SKIRINGSAL: Blindheim (1960).

OSEBERG TAPESTRY: Hougen (1940); Krafft (1956).

FIGURES OF GODS: Gjærder (1966); Grieg (1954).

HORSE CULT: Gjessing (1943).

CARVED STONES: Davidson (1942, 1950); Jacobsen (1933); Kermode (1907); Lindqvist (1941–2).

SERPENTS: Nordland (1949).

AXE AND HAMMER: Davidson (1965); Paulsen (1956).

SWASTIKA: Lechler (1935).

BURIAL MOUNDS: Brøgger (1937, 1945).

WEAPON SACRIFICE: Wilson (1965).

EGGJUM RUNES: Høst (1960).

TEMPLES: Boethius (1931); Bruun (1928); M. Olsen (1928); O. Olsen (1965).

UPPSALA: Lindqvist (1936, 1949).

JELLING: Dyggve (1942, 1948, 1954); Kornerup (1875).

ALMGREN, B.   1962   'Den osynlige gudomen', *Proxima Thule*, Stockholm, 53–71.

ALMGREN, O.   1927   *Hällristningar och Kultbruk,* Stockholm. (trans. S. Vrancken, *Nordische Fels-zeichnungen als religiöse Urkunden,* Frankfurt, 1934).

ALTHIN, C. A.   1945   *Studien zu den bronzezeitlichen Fels-zeichnungen von Skåne,* vol. I, Stockholm.

ANDERSEN, A.   1951   'Det femte store mosefund', *Kuml* I, 9–22.

ARBMAN, H.   1940   Birka, *Untersuchungen und Studien,* Stockholm.

                             1945   *Käringsjön,* Stockholm.

                             1961   *The Vikings,* London.

ARNE, T. J.   1931   'Skandinavische Holzkammergräber aus der Wikingerzeit in der Ukraine' *Acta Archaeologica* II, 285–302. (see also STOLPE)

ART OF THE WORLD   1961   'Art of the Stone Age', vol. 5 by H. G. Bandi and others (trans. from the German by A. E. Keep), London.

ARWIDSSON, G.   1942   *Valsgärde 6,* Uppsala.

                             1954   *Valsgärde 8,* Uppsala

BAGGE, A.   1950   (with L. Kaelas). *Die Funde aus Dolmen und Ganggräbern in Schonen, Schweden,* Stockholm.

BECK, H.   1964   'Einige vendelzeitliche Bilddenkmäler und die literarische Überlieferung', *Verlag d. Bayerischen Akad. d. Wissenschaften* (Phil/Hist.) VI, 1–50.

BECKER, C. J.   1962   'A Danish hoard containing Neolithic chisels', *Acta Archaeologica* XXXIII, 79–92.

BING-BERGEN, J.   1934   *Der Sonnenwagen von Trundholm* (*Führer zur Urgeschichte* XI), Leipzig.

BJÖRN, A.   1927   'Bidrag til den yngre Stenalder i Øst-Norge', *Universitets Oldsaksamlings årbok,* Oslo.

BLINDHEIM, C.   1960   'The Marketplace at Skiringsal', *Acta Archaeologica* XXXI, 83–100.

BOETHIUS, G.   1931   *Hallar, Tempel och Stavkyrker,* Stockholm.

BOSANQUET, R. C.   1922   'On an altar dedicated to the Alaisiagae', *Arch. Aeliana* (3rd series) XIX, 185–93.

Bowra, C. M. — 1962 — *Primitive Song,* London.

Broholm, H. C. — 1949 — (With W. P. Larsen and G. Skjerne) *The Lures of the Bronze Age,* Copenhagen.

Bruce-Mitford R. L. S. — 1949 — 'The Sutton Hoo Ship-Burial', *Proc. Suffolk Institute of Archaeology* XXV, 1–78.

1952 — 'The Snape Ship-Burial', *ibid.* XXVI, 1–26.

1964 — 'Excavations at Sutton Hoo in 1938' *ibid.* XXX, 1–43.

Brøgger, A. W. — 1937 — 'Gullalder', *Viking* I, 137–195.

1945 — 'Oseberggraven-Haugbrottet', *ibid.* VIII, 1–44.

Brøndsted, J. — 1936 — 'Danish Inhumation Graves of the Viking Age', *Acta Archaeologica* VII, 1936, 81–228.

1954 — *Guldhornene,* Copenhagen.

1957–59 — *Danmarks Oldtid* (3 vols. 2nd ed.), Copenhagen.

1960 — *The Vikings,* London.

Bruun, D. — 1928 — *Fortidsminder og Nutidshjem paa Island,* Copenhagen.

Campbell, J. — 1960 — *The Masks of God,* vol. I (Primitive Mythology), London.

Chatellier, P. du — 1908 — (with L. le Pontois). 'La sépulture Scandinave à barque de l'Ile de Groix', *Bulletin de la Société Arch. du Finistère* (Quimper), XXXV, 137–232.

Childe, V. G. — 1949 — *Prehistoric Communities of the British Isles* (3rd ed.), London

1962 — *The Prehistory of European Society,* London.

Crawford, O. G. S. — 1957 — *The Eye Goddess,* London.

Daniel, G. — 1963 — *The Megalith Builders of Western Europe* (2nd ed.), London.

DAVIDSON, H. R. E.

1942   'Sigurd in the Art of the Viking Age' *Antiquity* XVI, 216–36.

1950   'Gods and Heroes in Stone', *Early Cultures of North-West Europe (H. M. Chadwick Memorial Studies),* Cambridge, 123–39.

1964   *Gods and Myths of Northern Europe* (Harmondsworth, London).

1965   'Thor's Hammer', *Folklore* LXXVI, 1–15.
      (with S. Hawkes), 'The Finglesham Man', *Antiquity* XXXIX, 23–7.
      (with P. Gelling), *The Chariot of the Sun*. In the press.

DRESCHER, H.

1962   'Neue Untersuchungen am Sonnenwagen von Trundholm, *Acta Archaeologica* XXXIII, 39–62.

DRJUPEDAL, R.

1952   (with H. C. Broholm), 'Marcus Schnabel og Bronzealderfundet fra Grevensvænge', *Arbøger f. Oldkyndighed o. Historie*, 5–55.

DYGGVE, E.

1942   'La fouille par le Musée national danois du tertre royal sud à Jelling en 1941', *Acta Archaeologica* XIII, 65–97.

1948   'The Royal Barrows at Jelling', *Antiquity* XXII, 190–200.

1954   'Gorm's Temple and Harald's Stave-Church', *Acta Archaeologica* XXV, 221–39.

ELIADE, M.

1958   *Patterns in Comparative Religion* (trans. Sheed), London.

1964   Shamanism: *Archaic Techniques of Ecstasy* (trans. Trask from *Le Chamanism*, Paris, 1951), London.

EVANS, J. D.

1959   *Malta*, London.

FOX, SIR C. F.

1959   *Life and Death in the Bronze Age*, London.

Frobenius, L. 1923 *Das unbekannte Afrika,* Munich.

Gelling, P. (with H. R. E. Davidson) *The Chariot of the Sun.* In the press.

Gjessing, G. 1932 *Arktiske Helleristningen i Nord-Norge,* Oslo.

1942 'Une sépulture à haches en bateau norvégienne', *Acta Archaeologica* XIII, 215–23.

1943 'Hesten i forhistorisk Kunst og Kultus', *Viking* VII, 5–143.

1945 *Norges Steinalder,* Oslo.

Gjærder, P. 1966 'The Beard as an Iconographical Feature in the Viking Period', *Acta Archaeologica* XXXV, 95–114.

Glob, P. V. 1965 *Mosefolket,* Copenhagen

Green, C. 1963 *Sutton Hoo,* London.

Grieg, S. 1954 'Amuletter og Guldbilder', *Viking* XVIII, 157–209.

Grinsell, L. V. 1941 'The Boat of the Dead in the Bronze Age', *Antiquity* XV, 360–70.

1942 'The Kivik Cairn, Scania', *ibid.* 160–75.

Grønbech, V. 1931 *The Culture of the Teutons* (2 vols.), London/Copenhagen.

Hagberg, U. E. 1964 'Järnalderens offerfynd ur svensk perspektiv', *Tor* X, 222–39.

Hagen, A. 1955 'Vognen', *Viking* XIX, 9–47.

1965 *Rock Carvings in Norway,* Oslo.

1967 *Norway,* London.

Hallstrom, G. 1960 *Monumental Art of Northern Europe from the Stone Age* (2 vols.), Stockholm.

Hawkes, C. F. C. 1940 *The Prehistoric Foundations of Europe to the Mycenean Age,* London.

Hawkes, S. 1965 'The Finglesham Man', *Antiquity* XXXIX, 17–23.

HERTZ, R.   1960   *Death, and the Right Hand* (trans. Needham), London.

HINSCH, E.   1946   'En ny batgrav pa klassick grunn', *Viking* IX, 163–83.

HOLMQVIST, W.   1960   'The Dancing Gods', *Acta Archaeologica* XXXI, 101–27.

HØST, G.   1960   'To Runestudier', *Norsk Tidsskrift for Sprogvidenskap* XIX, 489–554.

HOUGEN, B.   1940   'Osebergfunnets Billedvev', *Viking* IV, 85–124.

INGSTAD, A. S.   1961   'Votive finds from the Northern Bronze Age', *Viking* XXV, 23–49.

JACOBSEN, L.   1933   *Evje-Stenen og Alstad-Stenen (Norske Oldfunn VI)*, Oslo.

JAMES, E. O.   1957   *Prehistoric Religion*, London.
   1959   *The Cult of the Mother Goddess*, London.

JANKUHN, H.   1936   'Zur Deutung des Moorfundes von Thorsberg' and 'Die Religionsgeschichtliche Bedeutung des Thorsberger Fundes', *Forschungen und Fortschritte* XII, 202, 365–66.
   1958   'Moorfunde', *Neue Ausgrabungen in Deutschland*, ed. Kramer, Berlin, 242–254.

KAELAS, L.   1955   'Dolmen und Ganggräber in Schweden', *Offa* XV, 5–24 (see also BAGGE).

KERMODE, P. A. C.   1907   *Manx Crosses*, London.

KLINDT-JENSEN, O.   1949   *Foreign Influences in Denmark's Early Iron Age (Acta Archaeologica XX)*.
   1957   *Bornholm i Folkevandringstiden*, Copenhagen, 83–6.
   1957   *Denmark before the Vikings*, London.
   1960   'Le chaudron de Gundestrup', *Analecta Romana Instituti Danici*, 45–66.

KNIGHT, W. F. J.   1932   'Maze Symbolism and the Trojan

Game', *Antiquity* VI, 445–58.

Kornerup, J.	1875	*Konghøiene i Jellinge,* Copenhagen.
Krafft, S.	1956	*Pictorial Weavings from the Viking Age* (trans. R. I. Christophersen), Oslo.
Kuhn, H.	1952	*Die Felsbilder Europas,* Stuttgart.
Lambrechts, P.	1942	*Contributions à l'étude des divinités celtiques,* Bruges.
Lechler, J.	1935	'Kreuz, Hakenkreuz und Irminsul', *Mannus* XXVIII, 345–73.
Lehman, K.	1910	'Grabhügel und Königshügel in nordischer Heidenzeit', *Zeitschrift f. deutsche Philologie* XLII, 1–15.
Levy, G. R.	1949	*The Gate of Horn,* London.
Lindqvist, S.	1936	*Uppsala Högar och Ottarshögen,* Stockholm.
	1941–2	*Gotlands Bildsteine* (2 vols.), Stockholm.
	1942	'The Boat Models from Roos Carr', *Acta Archaeologica* XIII, 235–42.
	1949	*Gamla Uppsala Fornminnen (Svenska Fornminnesplatser* XIII), Stockholm.
	1962	'Jättestenen fran Sanda och andra nyfunna Bildstenar', *Gotländskt Arkiv* XXXIV.
Lid, N.	1957	'The Paganism of the Norsemen', *Studies in Folklore in Honour of Stith Thomson,* Richmond (Indiana University Press), 241.
Mackeprang, M. B.	1935	'Menschendarstellungen aus der Eisenzeit Dänemarks', *Acta Archaeologica* VI, 228–49.
	1952	*De nordiske Guldbrakteater,* Aarhus.
Mathiassen, T.	1959	'Ravsmykker fra ældre Stenalder', *Aarbøger f. nord. Oldkyndighed,* 184–200.
Møhl-Hansen, U.	1954	'Første sikre spor af mennesker fra Interglacialtid, Danmark', *Aarbøger*

f. nord. Oldkyndighed, 100–26 (See also *ibid*. 1955, 133.)

NICOLAYSEN, N.   1882   *Langskibet fra Gokstad ved Sandefjord*, Christiania.

NORDÉN, A.   1939   'Le problème des "Bonhommes en Or"', *Acta Archaeologica* IX, 151–63.

NORDLAND, D.   1949   'Ormegarden', *Viking* XIII, 77–126.

NORLING-
CHRISTENSEN, H.   1946   'The Viksø Helmets', *Acta Archaeologica* XVII, 99–115.

OLSEN, M.   1914–24   *Norges Indskrifter med de Ældre Runer*, vol. III, 14–5, Copenhagen.

    1928   *Farms and Fanes of Ancient Norway*, Oslo.

OLSEN, O.   1965   'Hørg, Hov og Kirke', *Aarbøger f. nord. Oldkundighed*.

OLRIK, A.   1909   'At sidde på höj', *Danske Studier*, 1–10.

ØRSNES, M.   1963   'The Weapon Find in Ejsbøl Mose at Haderslev', *Acta Archaeologica* XXXIV, 232–41.

    1964   'Mosefund – stratigraft og kronologi', *Tor* X, 205–21.

OXENSTIERNA, COUNT E.   1956   *Die Goldhörner von Gallehus*, Lidingo.

    1965   *The Norsemen*, New York.

PAULSEN, P.   1956   *Axt und Kreuz in Nord- und Osteuropa*, Bonn.

POWELL, T. G. E.   1958   *The Celts*, London.

RAMSKOU, T.   1950   'Viking Age Cremation Graves in Denmark', *Acta Archaeologica* XXI, 137–82.

ROSENBERG, A. T.   1929   'Et Gudebillede fra Broncealderan', *Danske Studier*, 1–9.

SCHMID, W.   1934   'Der Kultwagen von Strettweg', *Führer zur Urgeschichte* XII, Leipzig.

SCHMIDT, W.   1912–55   *Der Ursprung der Gottesidee* (12 vols.), Münster in Westphalia.

SHETELIG, H.   1917   *Oseberg funnet* I, Oslo.
                           1940–54 *Viking Antiquities in Great Britain and Ireland* (4 vols), Oslo.

SJŒSTEDT-JONVAL, M.   1949   *Gods and Heroes of the Celts* (trans. M. Dillon), London.

SLOMANN, W.   1959   *Sætrangfundet (Norske Oldfunn* IX), Oslo.

SPROCKHOFF, E.   1954   'Nordische Bronzezeit und frühes Griechentum', *Jahrb. d. röm. germ. Zentralmuseums Mainz* I, 28–110.

                           1955   'Das bronzene Zierband von Kronshagen bei Kiel', *Offa* XIV, 5–120.

STENBERGER, M.   1956   'Tuna in Badelunda', *Acta Archaeologica* XXVII, 1–21.

                           1962   *Sweden,* London.

STOLPE, H.   1895   'Tunafyndet', *Ymer* XV, 219–34.

                           1927   (with T. J. Arne), *La Nécropole de Vendel,* Stockholm.

TARINGER, A.   1934   'Om kongevalg i Norge i sagatiden', *Norsk Historisk Tidsskrift* IX (series 5).

TURVILLE-PETRE, E. O.   1964   *Myth and Religion of the North,* London.

VAN DER POST, L.   1958   *The Lost World of the Kalahari,* London.

DE VRIES, J.   1956–7 *Altgermanische Religionsgeschichte* (2nd ed. 2 vols).

WERNER, J.   1951   'Ein langobardischer Schild von Ischl', *Bayerische Vorgeschichtsblätter* XVIII, 45–58.

WILSON, D.   1965   'Some Neglected Late Anglo-Saxon Swords', *Medieval Archaeology* IX, 50–1.

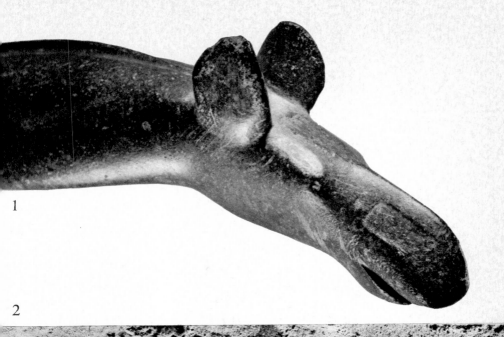

1

2

5

6

7

8

9

10

11

12

15

16

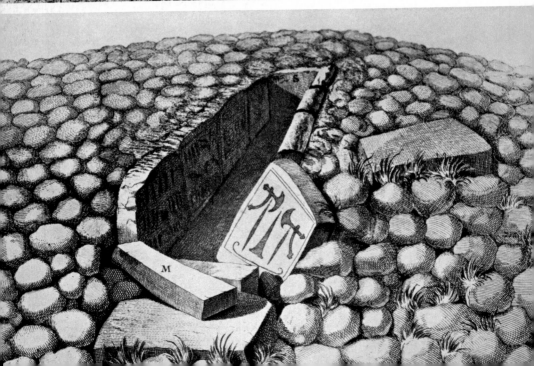

19

20

21

22

Følgende Metal figurer er ... opgravene i Sielland

nemlig 3de af denne Skikkelse

Disse nedenstaaende 2de er hinanden i alt aldeles lige, uden mindste forskiel, og fæste med Bronce op under Ladningen og paa figuren er ... ud ad, saaledes i paaldet med ... for kunde forestiller

Sue af samme figuren forestillet halv til.

... er ... ligt som i ... te del de form d'Ete.

Chr. Brandt.

23

24

25

27

28

29

30

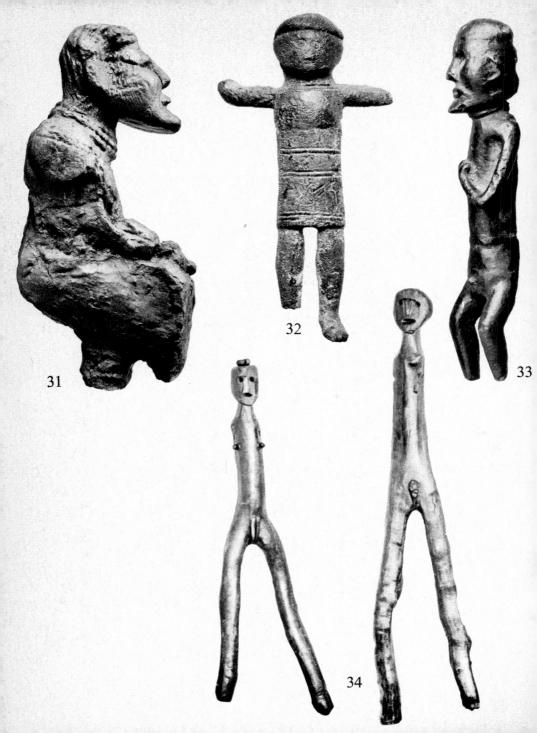

31   32   33   34

35

36

37

38 39

40

41

42

43　　　44

45

46

47

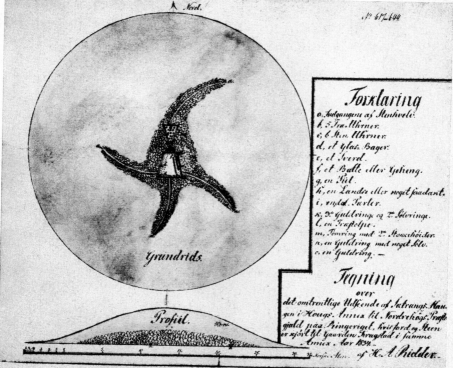

48

49

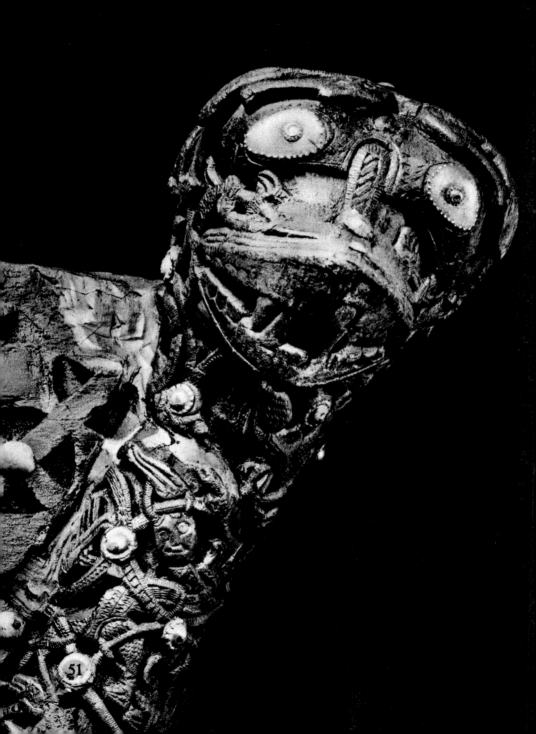

52

53

54

55

56 57

58 59 60 61

62 63

64

65

66

Notes on the Plates

1 Carved head of elk, forming part of axe-head of greenstone. From Alunda, Uppland, Sweden, probably an export from Karelia. Length 21 cm. Photo courtesy Statens Historiska Museum, Stockholm.

2 Rock carving at Nämforsen, Angermanland, Sweden, showing running elk. Photo (taken by night in 1963) courtesy Statens Historiska Museum, Stockholm.

3 Rock carving at Evenhus, N. Trøndelag, Norway, showing figure of elk with 'life-line'. Photo courtesy Videnskap. Oldsaksamling, Trondheim.

4 Rock carving at Strand, N. Trøndelag, Norway, showing whale and 'frame' figures. Photo courtesy Videnskap. Oldsaksamling, Trondheim.

5 Rock carving of horned human figure on skis, at Rødøy, Tjotta, Nordland, Norway. Length of carving 35.5 cm. Photo courtesy Videnskap. Oldsaksamling, Trondheim.

6 Human figure carved on axe of reindeer horn, found in Jordløse bog, Zealand, Denmark, probably from Kongemose culture. The man is in a recumbent posture, possibly bound, and may represent a shaman in a state of trance. Length approx. 17 cm. Photo courtesy National Museum, Copenhagen.

7 Dolmen at Skalstrup, Roskilde Vor Frue, Denmark, built over a seven-sided grave-chamber, with large cover-stone as roof. Photo courtesy National Museum, Copenhagen.

8 Dolmen near Haga, Orust, Bohuslän, Sweden. Photo Arvid Enqvist, courtesy Statens Historiska Museum, Stockholm.

9 Passage grave at Martofte, Hindsholm, N. Funen, Denmark, showing skeleton remains in grave chamber, which is more than 10 m. in length. Photo courtesy National Museum, Copenhagen.

10   Interior of passage grave, King Asker's Howe, Sprove Møn, Denmark. The chamber is more than 10 m. in length, and is entered by a passage 8 m. long. Photo courtesy National Museum, Copenhagen.

11   Grave at Skrelunda, Västergötland, showing grave chamber divided by holed partitions. Photo Andersen, 1936, courtesy Statens Historiska Museum, Stockholm.

12   Tree coffin in a howe, during excavation in 1921 of 'Storehøj' at Egtved, near Kolding, Jutland, Denmark. The coffin, which rested on a bed of stones, was about 2 m. long, made from a split and hollowed oak trunk. Inside was the outline of the body of a young woman and the cremated remains of a child about eight years old. The woman was clothed in jacket and short skirt, wrapped in a blanket, and lying on a cow-hide. Photo courtesy National Museum, Copenhagen.

13   Large ship-setting of stones beside the road at Gannarve, on the west coast of Gotland. The sea can be seen beyond the field. This, one of the largest stone 'ships', is about 29 m. in length, with 56 stones along one side and 54 on the other, and one large upright stone at either end. Photo courtesy Gotlands Fornsal, Visby.

14   Ship-setting in a wood at Gnisvärd, near Fröjel, Gotland, on the west coast. Photo courtesy Gotlands Fornsal, Visby.

15   Two slabs (nos 6 and 7) from the burial chamber at Kivik, Scania, Sweden. The stones have been restored and the designs painted, and they have been erected in position according to drawings made at the time of the discovery, in the eighteenth century. Photo courtesy Statens Historiska Museum, Stockholm.

16   Drawing of Kivik burial chamber in the centre of stone cairn, from a print of about 1780. The first slab, shown here, was lost soon afterwards. The cairn of stones which covered the grave was 75 m. in diameter, larger than any other grave of the Bronze Age known in Sweden. Photo courtesy Statens Historiska Museum, Stockholm.

17   Rock carving at Fossum, Tanum, Bohuslän, Sweden, showing, *inter alia*, ships, axe-bearers, a man with a spear, a *lur*-blower, an archer. Photo C.

Claesson, 1938, courtesy Statens Historiska Museum, Stockholm.

18 Rock carving at Tegneby, Tanum, Bohuslän, Sweden, showing ships, disc-men with axes and bird-heads, footprint, and worshippers round a sun-disc(?). Photo courtesy Statens Historiska Museum, Stockholm.

19 Ritual axe from Västerås, Västmanland, Sweden. It weighs 3.5 kg. and is too large and heavy for practical use. Photo courtesy Statens Historiska Museum, Stockholm.

20 'Sun-chariot' from Trundholm, north Zealand, Denmark. Found in fragments and reconstructed. It may originally have been drawn by two horses. The horse is of bronze, and the disc is gold-plated on one side, and ornamented on both with spiral patterns. The disc is about 26 cm. in diameter, and length of wagon and horse is 60 cm. Photo courtesy National Museum, Copenhagen.

21 Wheeled cauldron of bronze, with small bird figures, and hanging ornaments on the rim which rattle as it moves. Found containing cremated human bones in a tree coffin in 'Trushøj', Skallerup, south Jutland. Height approx. 31 cm. Photo courtesy National Museum, Copenhagen.

22 House urn from Ansarve, Tofta, Gotland. Height 29 cm. Photo courtesy Gotlands Fornsal, Visby.

23 Drawing of figures from Grevens Vænge, Zealand, Denmark, by C. Brandt (d. 1780), about 1778. The drawing was preserved in the Royal Library at Copenhagen, and according to this, and another contemporary drawing by Marcus Schnabel, the find originally consisted of two axe-bearers, three girl acrobats, and one standing female (?) figure. Only two of these six figures, an axe-bearer (without his axe) and one acrobat, reached the National Museum. The man in the horned helmet is approx. 10.2 cm. high, and the bending figure 4.8 cm. from feet to head. Photo courtesy National Museum, Copenhagen.

24 Two figures from different sites in Scania, Sweden. The man in the helmet is one of a pair of figures from a hoard at Stockmult, belonging to the Early Bronze Age; he is about 15 cm. in height. The female figure is from

St Olov, and belongs to the Late Bronze Age. She wears a neckring and short skirt. Photo courtesy Statens Historiska Museum, Stockholm.

25 Two figures from Fardål, north Jutland, Denmark, from the Late Bronze Age. The woman in short corded skirt and necklace, her hair in a short plait, is believed to represent the fertility goddess. She seems from her posture to be driving, and one reconstruction of the group shows her driving the serpent. An alternative grouping by Althin makes her feed the serpent from her breast, the nipple of which is grasped by her left hand. The height of the woman is about 5 cm. Photo courtesy National Museum, Copenhagen.

26 The man from a peat bog at Tollund, north Jutland, in 1950, shown lying as he was found, dressed in a cloak and pointed leather cap, with a rope round his neck. Photo courtesy National Museum, Copenhagen.

27 A woman's grave in a small inhumation cemetery at Juellinge, near Nakshov, Denmark. She was buried with gold and silver ornaments, and near her head was a wooden workbox, with scissors, knife, comb and other possessions. She had two fine glass beakers, two drinking horns, and a large bronze cauldron (at one end of the grave) which had held a drink made of barley, red whortleberries, cranberries and bog myrtle. A ladle was provided, and the woman held a bronze wine strainer in her right hand. Beside the cauldron lay joints of meat from an ox and a young pig. Photo courtesy National Museum, Copenhagen.

28 Decorated wagon, reconstructed from fragments recovered from Præstegaardsmose, Dejbjerg, west Jutland, with parts of a similar wagon found at the same time. The remains lay in two heaps in the middle of the bog, surrounded by wooden stakes. The wagon was of ash wood, with fittings of gilded bronze, and there was a single seat of wood and leather. The second wagon was similar to the first, but a little wider, and with four-spoked wheels. Length of wagon about 176 cm.; width 103 cm. Photo courtesy National Museum, Copenhagen.

29 Circular plate over base of bowl from Gundestrup, north Jutland. It shows a man about to stab a bull, with two dogs attacking the animal and a third lying on the ground. The bull's horns are lost. Base about

24 cm. in diameter. Photo courtesy National Museum, Copenhagen.

30 One of the seven plates from the outside of the Gundestrup bowl; the eighth is missing. This plate shows a male deity (?) grasping a small figure in each hand, and the figures in turn grasp boars. Approx. 23 × 18 cm. Photo courtesy National Museum, Copenhagen.

31 Statuette of hollow bronze of a male figure in helmet (?) and either tunic or coat of mail. Found together with a bronze cauldron holding cremated human remains, a sword, two spears, a knife and a shield, in 'Frøihov', Romerike, Norway, in 1865. Some runic symbols are still visible on the body. Height 7.2 cm. Photo courtesy Universitets Oldsaksamling, Oslo.

32 Wooden figure of man from a bog at Rude Eskildstrup, Zealand, wearing a triple neckring of gold, of a type known from the late fifth century AD. Height about 41 cm. Photo courtesy National Museum, Copenhagen.

33 Hollow statuette of bronze, with open back, of naked male figure, with neckring and belt. His carefully modelled face resembles that of the larger wooden figure from Rude Eskildstrup. Found at Bregnebjerg, Funen. Several similar male figures have been discovered in this area. Height 12.6 cm. Photo courtesy National Museum, Copenhagen.

34 Male and female figures of wood, after restoration. Found in a bog on Aukemper Moor, Braak, Kresi Eulen, Schleswig, near a stone enclosure with carbon and potsherds which might have been a cult place. Height of male figure 2.75 m.; female 2.27 m. Photo courtesy Schleswig-Holsteinisches Landesmuseum.

35 Bronze heads of bulls from cauldrons found in Denmark. The two larger heads are from Sophienburg bog in Zealand, and the small head from Rå bog, west Zealand. The large head on the right is about 24 cm. high. Photo courtesy National Museum, Copenhagen.

36 Gold bracteate, *c.* AD 685, from unknown site probably in Denmark, showing youth in horned helmet, horse, bird, and swastika. Approx. diameter 2.87 cm. Photo courtesy Universitets Oldsaksamling, Oslo.

37 Buckle of gilded bronze from the Anglo-Saxon cemetery at Finglesham,
Kent, with bosses and rivets encircled with gold wire. It shows a naked
male figure in a horned helmet and belt, holding a spear in each hand.
Length of buckle 8 cm. Photo courtesy Mrs Sonia Hawkes.

38 Small plate of gold foil, one of a series of sixteen found on the farm at
Hange, Klepp, Rogaland, Norway. At the neighbouring farm of Tu,
a runic stone has a carving of a male and a female figure, which bear some
resemblance to the man and woman on the small gold plates. About
1.6 × 1.5 cm. Photo courtesy Historisk Museum, Bergen.

39 Small hollow figure of gold plate, with part of back missing, from Trønninge, Holbæk, Denmark. In the form of a sitting man, his hair carefully
parted in a knot on the nape of his neck, elaborately clothed. At the back
his cloak resembles feathers. Height 1.95 cm. Photo courtesy National
Museum, Copenhagen.

40 Helmet plate from grave I at Vendel, showing warrior with eagle helmet,
accompanied by eagle and raven (?), and confronted by a serpent. Height
5.3 cm. Photo E. Oxenstierna, *Die Nordgermanen*.

41 Set of four bronze dies for making helmet plates, found at Torslunda,
Öland. These are of cast bronze, with carved details. 1:1. Photo courtesy
Statens Historika Museum, Stockholm.

42 Helmet discovered in a burial mound at Benty Grange farm, Derbyshire,
in 1848. The iron framework had formed the internal supports for the
helmet casing, and the figure of a boar formed the crest. After cleaning,
the boar was found to be a bronze figure, decorated with plates of gilded
silver and minute silver studs, also gilt. Length of boar 9.5 cm. The helmet was cleaned and elucidated in the British Museum, with the co-
operation of the Sheffield authorities. Photo courtesy the Trustees of the
British Museum, London.

43 Stone sphere from Pilungs, Mästerby, Gotland, with swastika motif as
decoration. Diameter approx. 55 cm. Photo courtesy Gotlands Fornsal,
Visby.

44 Silver ornamental disc, partially gilded, from Gjone, Kvelde, Vestfold, Norway. Found in a grave in a large mound forming part of a small cemetery. Probably fifth century. Remains of a silver loop on the back suggest that it was worn as a pendant. Approx. diameter 4.25 cm. Photo courtesy Universitets Oldsaksamling, Oslo.

45 Cremation urn from Linnum, Brunlanes, Vestfold, Norway, with swastika decoration. Found in a mound with burnt bones and other objects. Early fourth or late third century. Height 13.6 cm. Photo courtesy Universitets Oldsaksamling, Oslo.

46 Large stone found in pieces under the floor of the church in Sanda, Gotland, during restoration in 1954. Believed to date from the early sixth century. The stone has the usual whirling disc motif, and a ship, but is unique in that it bears a tree motif and the head of a dragon above the ship. Max. height 340 cm. Photo courtesy Gotlands Fornsal, Visby.

47 Plan and cross-section of tumulus at Sætrang, Norway, showing stone cairn and burial chambers. From a water-colour painting by H. A. Ridder, done in 1834, when the mound was excavated. The mound was 20 m. in diameter and 4 m. high. Photo courtesy Dr W. Slomann, Oslo.

48 The three great burial mounds, believed to be royal graves, at Gamle Uppsala, Sweden, beside the medieval church. From a nineteenth-century painting by C. J. Billmork. Photo courtesy Statens Historiska Museum, Stockholm.

49 Tynwald Hill, Isle of Man. From a drawing in the Manx Museum, about 1774, attributed to Godfrey, who was probably working for Grose at this time. Photo courtesy Manx Museum, Douglas.

50 The ship-burial at Gokstad, Vestfold, Norway, showing the ship in the mound during excavation. From a photograph of 1880. Photo courtesy Universitets Oldsaksamling, Oslo.

51 Carved animal-head from one of the corner posts of 'Gustafson's sledge', one of the three decorated sledges discovered in the ship-burial at Oseberg, Vestfold, and restored. This sledge was made of beech-wood, and elabo-

rately carved. All four heads are different, each grotesque and menacing. Length of sledge 2.25 m. Photo courtesy Viking Ship Museum, Oslo.

52 Stone (no. 1), from Lärbro Tängelgårda, Gotland, found in 1861. Some of its scenes have unusual features. In the top panel is a battle scene, dom-inated by eagles. In the next panel a (dead?) man is carried on an eight-legged horse; in the third, a rider is welcomed by a woman with a horn and by men holding rings. The usual ship is below. Height of stone (now in the Statens Historiska Museum) 269 cm. Width of head 127 cm.; base 144 cm. Photo courtesy Statens Historiska Museum, Stockholm.

53 Stone (no. 8) from Ardre, Gotland. This is covered with a number of small scenes, arranged in a different way from the usual series of panels, and not satisfactorily interpreted. The top panel shows a rider on an eight-legged horse, and the rounded object on the left is probably a hall. Some of the scenes below may be connected with the god Thor. Height 210 cm., width of upper part 129 cm. Photo H. Faith-Ell, 1931, courtesy Statens Historiska Museum, Stockholm.

54 Top panel from stone (no. 1) from Hunninge, Klinte, Gotland. This shows rider with spear, flying figure above, warriors fighting, and woman with horn. Found in 1860. Height of complete stone 284 cm.; width of head 125 cm. Photo courtesy Gotlands Fornsal, Visby.

55 One of two hog-back tombstones, now built into floor of the church at Gosforth, Cumberland. Both are much worn, but have clearly been carv-ed by a gifted sculptor. The panel at the side shows two human figures struggling with serpents, which are entwined round their limbs. At each end a human figure stands in a doorway, one with arms outstretched, the other carrying a staff. It has been suggested that these represent the crucified and risen Christ, but if this is a Christian memorial, it is a very uncon-ventional one. The stone was discovered during restoration of the church in 1896, under the north-east corner of the earlier twelfth-century nave. Photo B. C. Clayton, by kind permission of the Society of Antiquaries.

56 Halton Cross, Lancashire. The top of this has been broken off, and the shaft is much worn. At the top is a stylized tree, with two birds on the branches. Below, a figure, taken to be the hero Sigurd the Volsung, roasts slices of the dragon's heart with his thumb in his mouth, as on a number

of stones in the Isle of Man. Below this, a smith with hammer upraised, the bellows, and a headless body. Height of shaft 117 cm. Photo B. C. Clayton, by kind permission of the Society of Antiquaries.

57 Cross shaft from Andreas, Isle of Man, showing a man in a pointed cap, bound in fetters. On the other side there is a picture of Sigurd killing the dragon and roasting the heart. The shaft is much damaged and the edges have been chipped away, probably when built into the church wall. Discovered in 1885, used as a headstone for a modern grave. 68.5 × 41 cm. Photo courtesy Manx Museum, Douglas.

58 Small silver figure of a man in a horned helmet, carrying sword and rod (?). Probably an amulet. In grave no. 571 in the cemetery at Birka, Sweden. Height 2.9 cm. Photo courtesy Statens Historiska Museum, Stockholm.

59 Cast bronze figure of a seated man. The figure is phallic, and has been taken for the god Freyr. He wears a pointed cap, and grasps his beard with one hand. From Rällinge, Södermanland, Sweden. Height 7 cm. Photo courtesy Statens Historiska Museum, Stockholm.

60 Bronze figure seated on a chair, with pointed cap, holding his beard, which turns into a cross-shaped hammer. Taken to represent the god Thor. Found in 1817 on the farm Eyraland in Akureyri, north Iceland. Thought to date from about AD 1000. Height 6.7 cm. Photo Reykjavik Museum.

61 Bone figure, found at Lund, Sweden. The beard seems to be plaited, and is grasped in both hands. On the flat back of the figure is a pattern in circles which has been thought to be the outline of a hammer on a loop. Height 4.7 cm. Photo R. Blomqvist, Kulturhistoriska Museet, Lund.

62 Silver figure of man on horseback, from grave no. 825 in the cemetery at Birka, Sweden. One of a pair. Length 3.2 cm. Photo courtesy Statens Historiska Museum, Stockholm.

63 Silver figure of woman with horn resembling those on the Gotland stones. From Klinta, Öland. Height: 2.7 cm. Photo courtesy Statens Historiska Museum, Stockholm.

64 Stone discovered at Gosforth Church, Cumberland, in 1882, now built into wall inside the church. The figure in the boat is raising a hammer, and is thought to be the god Thor, with the giant Hymir as his companion, fishing for the World Serpent. Fish cluster round the bait, which according to the written sources was an ox-head, and the serpent may be represented by the coils above the boat. The stone is red sandstone, and measures 68.5 × 33 cm. Photo B. C. Clayton, by kind permission of the Society of Antiquaries.

65 Upright memorial stone at Altuna, Sweden, viewed from the side. The figure in the boat raising a hammer is thought to be Thor fishing for the serpent, which is seen below. No clear interpretation of the scene above has been put forward, but on the analogy of the Gotland stones it might represent a rider being challenged on his arrival at the door of the Other World; above the gate is an eagle. The runic inscriptions state that the stone was erected by three brothers for their father and a fourth brother who died by fire. It is dated to the early eleventh century. Height approx. 242 cm. Photo courtesy Statens Historiska Museum, Stockholm.

66 Central part of runic stone from Eggjum, Sogn, Norway, showing outline of horse between the two lines of runes. The inscription is long and very complicated, and appears to refer to magic rites associated with the dead. Found in 1917, and thought to have been placed above a grave, although no human remains were found. Photo courtesy Historiska Museet, Bergen.

67 Two of the most elaborate of the Thor hammers, made of silver, with filigree decoration. The hammer on the chain is from Erikstorp, Odeshög, Ostergotland, Sweden, and was found with a hoard of treasure, the latest coins of which were dated 1014–16. The hammer on the left is from Kabbarg, Barat, Scania, Sweden, also from a hoard. Both have hawk or eagle faces with round, staring eyes, and the lower part of the hammer forms a kind of beard below the face. The chain is gripped by two dragon or serpent heads. Actual size. Photo Statens Historiska Museum, Stockholm.

68 Stave church and bell-tower, Borgund, Norway. Twelfth century. Photo Carl Normanns, Hamar.